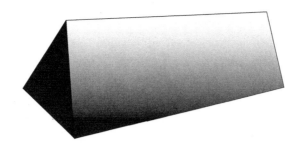

W9-CHG-303

DADD

PRISM SERIES

Volume 7

A Guide to Teaching Students With Autism Spectrum Disorders

by Darlene E. Perner
and Monica E. Delano

A Publication of the Division
on Autism and Developmental Disabilities
of the Council for Exceptional Children

Council for **Exceptional Children**
The voice and vision of special education

Table of Contents

Editors

Darlene E. Perner, Ed.D.
Department of Exceptionality Programs
Bloomsburg University of Pennsylvania
400 East 2nd Street
Bloomsburg, Pennsylvania 17815

Monica E. Delano, Ph.D.
Department of Special Education
College of Education and Human Development
University of Louisville
2301 S. 3rd Street
Louisville, Kentucky 40208

Contributors

Ruth Aspy, Ph.D.
The Ziggurat Group
5232 Village Creek, Suite 200
Plano, Texas 75093

Amy Bixler Coffin, M.A.
Ohio Center for Autism and Low Incidence (OCALI)
470 Glenmont Avenue
Columbus, Ohio 43214

Monica E. Delano, Ph.D.
Department of Special Education
College of Education and Human Development
University of Louisville
2301 S. 3rd Street
Louisville, Kentucky 40208

Barry Grossman, Ph.D.
The Ziggurat Group
5232 Village Creek, Suite 200
Plano, Texas 75093

Jill Hudson, M.S., CCLS
Ohio Center for Autism and Low Incidence (OCALI)
470 Glenmont Avenue
Columbus, Ohio 43214

Kara Hume, Ph.D.
Frank Porter Graham Child Development Institute
University of North Carolina at Chapel Hill
517 S. Greensboro
Carrboro, North Carolina 27510

Renee A. Lake, M.S.Ed., M.A.
The Ohio State University
PAES Building, 305 W. 17th Ave.
Columbus, Ohio 43210

G. Rich Mancil, Ph.D., BCBA
670 Wakefield Street
Bowling Green, Kentucky 42103

Brenda Smith Myles, Ph.D.
The Ziggurat Group
5232 Village Creek, Suite 200
Plano, Texas 75093

Robert C. Pennington, Ph.D.
Department of Special Education
College of Education and Human Development and
  Kentucky Autism Training Center
University of Louisville
2301 S. 3rd Street
Louisville, Kentucky 40208

Darlene E. Perner, Ed.D.
Department of Exceptionality Programs
Bloomsburg University of Pennsylvania
400 East 2nd Street
Bloomsburg, Pennsylvania 17815

Martha E. Snell, Ph.D.
Department of Curriculum and Instruction, and Special Education
Curry School of Education
University of Virginia
Charlottesville, Virginia 22904

Maureen Walsh, Ed.D.
Department of Exceptionality Programs
Bloomsburg University of Pennsylvania
400 East 2nd Street
Bloomsburg, Pennsylvania 17815

Kelly Whalon, Ph.D.
School of Special Education
School Psychology and Early Childhood Studies
Center for Excellence in Early Childhood Studies
University of Florida
Gainesville, Florida 32611

Peggy J. Schaefer Whitby, Ph.D.
Department of Special Education and Early Childhood Education
University of Nevada, Las Vegas
4505 S Maryland Pkwy.
Las Vegas, Nevada 89154

Barbara A. Wilson, Ed.D.
Department of Exceptionality Programs
Bloomsburg University of Pennsylvania
400 East 2nd Street
Bloomsburg, Pennsylvania 17815

Barbara Yingling Wert, Ph.D.
Department of Exceptionality Programs
Bloomsburg University of Pennsylvania
400 East 2nd Street
Bloomsburg, Pennsylvania 17815

Foreword

My introduction to children with autism was in the 1970s as an undergraduate at the University of California, Santa Barbara. As a research assistant for luminaries in the field (Ivar Lovaas, Bob Koegel, and Laura Schreibman) and their doctoral students, I worked with children with autism who were institutionalized in a state facility. In the 1980s, I worked with Phil Strain and an extraordinary team of individuals who were developing one of the first inclusive classrooms—the LEAP preschool model. Children with autism were integrated into classrooms for typically developing preschoolers, and parents were trained to facilitate their children's development. My research focused on teaching language, play, and social communication skills to children with autism often with the help of their peers. In recent years, I have examined the evidence base for teaching practices in autism with a special focus on early childhood. In reading *A Guide to Teaching Students With Autism Spectrum Disorders,* edited by Darlene Perner and Monica Delano, it is clear that we have made amazing progress over the past 40 years.

Children with autism spectrum disorders (ASD) present many challenges to teachers. Children with ASD tend to be socially withdrawn or socially inept. Most have limited communication skills. Sometimes they are overly sensitive to their sensory environment and sometimes they seem oblivious to important cues in their environment. They are likely to exhibit behavior problems, including tantrums, stereotypic behavior, or aggressive behavior. The field has shown that many of these characteristics can be ameliorated through early intervention. As a consequence, many more children with ASD can be integrated successfully into general education classrooms or less restrictive educational settings. Although such placements may be the source of considerable anxiety among many educators, there is valuable information to be shared that will help teachers. This book offers a useful resource for special educators and general educators striving to ensure that all their students are successful learners.

The authors build from a common assumption—that students with autism can learn a broad array of functional skills. The underlying premise is that students should be explicitly taught a full range of social, self-help, language, reading, writing, and math skills, similar to their typically developing classmates. The focus is on explicit teaching. Brief chapters provide teachers with information about how to approach the tasks of determining what to teach and how to teach, often with clearly outlined steps for doing so.

Teachers would be hard pressed to find a more practical book for helping them learn how to include students with ASD in their classrooms and provide them with the instruction needed to help them succeed.

In reading this volume I encountered a set of expectations that I found refreshing. The primary expectation is that students with ASD are capable of learning—learning a full gamut of skills that are needed to function in today's society. For the most part, the authors resist pointing out what makes students with ASD "special." Instead, they focus on strategies and teaching procedures that have shown great promise in helping children who often are difficult to teach. One reason readers should appreciate this book is that it covers a myriad of teaching tactics that have general applicability to all students who experience learning difficulties. Although the authors cite literature on applications to children with autism and point out some of the common characteristics of autism that often interfere with learning, one should appreciate the contributions of special education to the teaching professions generally.

Perhaps this volume exemplifies the role of special education as a driving force for improving educational attainment generally and for maximizing success in academic settings. The idea of differentiating instruction quickly and adeptly to meet the needs of individual learners is slowly becoming the new, universal expectation for all educators. Moreover, the contributing authors are sharing assessment tools that are being developed to help teachers quickly identify students who are not making progress in learning situations, teaching tactics that can be employed to remedy learning difficulties, and progress monitoring tools to assess if adequate learning is being accomplished.

Reading this book, many teachers may be struck by the expectation that children with ASD can and most often should be educated along with fellow classmates who are developing typically. This expectation is not a matter of placement. Simply placing students with ASD in general education classrooms is not sufficient. They need to be fully included; they need to experience a sense of belonging like all other children. That expectation is transmitted from teachers to students and to others. Likewise, adding an instructional aide for the student is not sufficient, as that may insulate the student with ASD from fellow classmates. As pointed out in this volume, the provision of effective instruction is critically important. Also, there is ample evidence that typically developing peers can play a valuable role as models, as assistants, and as reinforcing agents, but not unless they are taught and prompted to do so. Thus, the classroom must be structured as an environment that reflects high expectations and provides sufficient support from teaching staff and from peers.

The contributing authors of the 13 chapters included in this volume tantalize the reader with the state-of-the-art knowledge of how the teaching profession should be applied to students with ASD. Because the chapters are brief they do not include a comprehensive review of the literature in each of the areas covered. Instead, the authors present practical information that is meant to guide teaching practices. They also do a fine job of providing lists of resources that provide more in-depth information. Most importantly, they raise the bar for a basic understanding of how to educate students with ASD, what constitutes effective instructional strategies, and how to promote access to the general education curriculum. Realizing that a cornucopia of tools exists to help educate students with ASD should lower the anxiety of teachers who may have limited experience in teaching students with ASD in their classrooms. They should look forward to the opportunity to maximize the potential of all their students and this book will provide a valuable resource. This book highlights the knowledge that we have gained in recent decades. Students with autism are capable of accomplishing much more than we thought possible 40 years ago. It is important that educators have the tools and expectations to put their students on a trajectory that enables them to fit in and contribute to society.

Howard Goldstein, Ph.D.
Professor of Human Development and Family Science
The Ohio State University

Preface

The intent of this Division on Autism and Developmental Disabilities (DADD) Prism Series, Volume 7 book is to provide a user-friendly guide for special and general education teachers, teacher candidates who will soon enter the field, and all who are responsible for the education of students with autism spectrum disorders (ASD). There are a number of factors that influenced us in editing this DADD Prism Series Volume 7 book. First the Prism series is written for teachers and the content is intended to be relevant to classroom practice. Second, we wanted this book to be accessible and user-friendly. The chapters are concise, provide "real life" examples, and list resources for further study. Third, and most important, we wanted to present research-based strategies that are effective when teaching students with ASD. In cases where there is not sufficient research with students with ASD to guide practice (e.g., providing access to the general education curriculum), authors described how practices that are effective with other populations of students can be adapted for learners with ASD. All the contributors to this book have taught students with ASD and other developmental disabilities, and are currently involved in teacher training at universities, professional conferences, or in school districts. We share these research-based strategies because we value teachers and all the students we teach.

This book is composed of 13 chapters, divided into three sections: *Getting Started, Effective Instructional Strategies*, and *Access to the General Education Curriculum*. Section I, *Getting Started*, contains three chapters. In Chapter 1, Robert C. Pennington discusses how to set up instructional environments that will meet the learning needs and preferences of students. Strategies are discussed that include not only classroom arrangement, but also instructional and structural supports such as visuals, schedules, and direct instruction. Brenda Smith Myles, Amy Bixler Coffin, Jill Hudson, Renee A. Lake, Barry Grossman, and Ruth Aspy address the question "How do I determine what to teach?" in Chapter 2. A number of assessments and models are described to assist teachers in comprehensive program planning for students with ASD and other developmental disabilities. In Chapter 3, Barbara A. Wilson addresses the question, "How do I know if my students are learning?" A detailed description with examples is presented focusing on collecting and analyzing data that will provide on-going measurement of student progress and instructional effectiveness.

Section II, *Effective Instructional Strategies*, consists of five chapters. Kara Hume provides an overview of systematic instruction in Chapter 4. She describes evidence-based strategies including direct instruction, response prompting, and discrete trial training. Next, in Chapter 5, Robert C. Pennington and G. Rich Mancil focus on functional communication training to assist teachers in replacing challenging behaviors with communication skills that serve the same function. Conducting a functional behavior assessment is described and a case example is illustrated. In addition G. Rich Mancil explains naturalistic interventions in Chapter 6. He describes four strategies: modeling, mand-modeling, time delay, and incidental teaching. Developing and increasing social skills is an important instructional area for students with ASD and developmental disabilities. In Chapter 7, Monica E. Delano, Kelly Whalon, and Barbara Y. Wert highlight two evidence-based strategies, peer-mediated instruction, and video modeling. Toileting abilities are crucial for any student, but developing these skills can often be challenging both for the student and the teacher. In Chapter 8, Martha E. Snell and Monica E. Delano provide advice and examples on selecting a teaching method, resolving issues prior to toilet training, and implementing a systematic schedule.

Section III, *Access to the General Education Curriculum*, contains five chapters. Darlene E. Perner and Maureen Walsh team up in the next two chapters. They describe collaboration skills that are needed when general and special educators work together to instruct students in the general education classroom. In Chapter 9 Walsh and Perner introduce co-teaching and identify the beginning steps to create a successful co-teaching environment for teachers and their students. In Chapter 10 they define differentiated instruction and focus on one strategy that is commonly used in inclusive classrooms, tiered instruction. An example of tiered instruction that was developed by co-teachers is illustrated in this chapter. Developing academic skills is critical, but research is just beginning to address teaching core content to students with ASD and developmental disabilities. Monica E. Delano collaborates with Kelly Whalon (Chapter 11) and Robert C. Pennington (Chapter 12) to describe strategies to enhance students' reading and writing. They provide many examples and classroom applications. In the last chapter (Chapter 13), Peggy J. Schaefer Whitby discusses teaching mathematics to students with high functioning autism. She describes the explicit instruction model and two evidence-based methodologies, the concrete-representational-abstract approach and strategy instruction. Teachers can use these approaches to increase students' conceptual understanding of mathematical processes.

Finally, we thank the authors of this Prism 7 series book for their outstanding contributions and collaboration. We appreciate your support as well as the support of DADD and all the teachers and students we have had the opportunity to work with in schools and universities, and in our personal lives. It is our hope that this book will assist you in supporting and teaching students with ASD and with other developmental disabilities.

Section I

Getting Started

Environmental Arrangement

Robert C. Pennington

When designing a classroom environment to include a student with autism spectrum disorders (ASD), the teacher must first consider the environmental arrangement. Through careful planning, features of the student's educational environment can be structured to both support the student's skill acquisition and reduce challenging behavior. Teachers can provide frequent opportunities to respond, increase the predictability of daily routines, and decrease the influence of competing sensory stimuli during instruction. Building the optimal instructional environment involves making decisions related to the physical layout of the classroom, the placement of preferred items within the classroom, the use of antecedent prompts and visual supports, the temporal structure of activities, and the selection of appropriate instructional arrangements.

These critical programming decisions are addressed within the Individuals With Disabilities Education Improvement Act (2004) and can be documented as supplementary aids and services in the individualized education program (IEP). Supplementary aids and services are comprised of any support, program modification, or accommodation that is provided to a student to help them achieve annual goals, to access the general education curriculum, and to be educated with peers without disabilities (Heward, 2009). Environmental supports can contribute greatly to the education of persons with ASD and therefore should be documented in the IEP to ensure their inclusion in the educational program.

Physical Layout of the Classroom

Teachers must first consider the safety of all students when designing the physical layout of the classroom and remove any visual barriers that would provide students the opportunity to engage in problem behavior without intervention. For example, some students with ASD may engage in elopement (i.e., running out of the classroom; Perrin, Perrin, Hill, & DiNovi, 2008). Therefore, there should a clear line of sight from every point in the classroom to every accessible window and door. Similarly, teachers must be able to monitor and restrict access to dangerous materials, edibles, and allergens. Some students with ASD may have a decreased awareness of the dangers these materials present and need protection until appropriate safety skills can be taught. Additionally, students may be seated in positions that place them at a decreased proximity to stimuli (e.g., open doors, food items, computer) that may trigger problem behavior. Though not a permanent solution, these simple adjustments in the environment can result in significant reductions in problem behavior.

Second, teachers should design the classroom to accommodate a variety of instructional arrangements (e.g., one-to-one [1:1], small group, large group). For example, teachers may provide seating arrangements that offer opportunities for students to work with their peers and engage in observational learning, while also offering areas for teachers to provide intensive systematic instruction (e.g., discrete trial instruction, incidental teaching) in 1:1 instructional arrangements. To increase the predictability of instructional routines, teachers should maintain consistency in the types of programming that occur in these areas. For example, a teacher may place a small kidney shaped table in the back of the room that is designated for small group instruction. Students may deliver stronger performance as they learn the expectations associated with each instructional area.

Third, teachers should arrange instructional environments in ways that facilitate interaction. Play, leisure, and instructional areas should require students to share materials, ask others for access to materials, and sit together in close proximity. Activities should be designed that involve students working together. For example, a teacher may divide a set of puzzle pieces between two students and ask them to complete it together, or a teacher may provide three students with one calculator to complete a math task. Certainly, many students with ASD will require explicit instruction in communication and turn-taking skills, but the first step will involve providing opportunities in which instruction can occur.

Finally, teachers must consider the impact of distracting stimuli on students' acquisition and performance of skills. Researchers have suggested that students with ASD may have atypical responses to sensory input. These stimuli (e.g., loud air conditioners, radios, honking cars, flashing computer screens), which can be aversive or reinforcing, may capture students' attention during instructional tasks and impede learning. Determining the impact of environmental stimuli on each student's distractibility is highly individualized and may be assessed by asking the student, observing the student's response to the stimuli, and by directly manipulating the environment (e.g., change in seating arrangement) and subsequently observing the student's response to the change. Once a source of distraction is determined, the teacher may reduce its impact by removing it, decreasing its proximity to the student, or by changing the student's position so that it is no longer in his/her visual field. Gradually, the teacher may reintroduce the distracting stimulus to ensure the student is learning in an environment congruent with real world contexts.

Placement of Preferred Items

The placement of preferred items within the instructional environment is critical to the success of any program. Free access to reinforcing items can distract students from instruction and may compete with the reinforcers used by teachers during instructional tasks. For example, a student might have difficulty understanding why he must complete a challenging task to earn a token when he can just walk to the teacher's desk and take a piece of candy. At the beginning of the year, teachers should limit access to reinforcers so students can acquire the skills necessary to obtain them (e.g., requesting, task completion). Once students acquire appropriate requesting, waiting, and self-management skills, teachers may gradually increase the availability of preferred items within the student's environment.

Teachers may also consider strategically placing preferred items in the environment to promote communication. For instance, teachers may "salt" a play area with preferred toys by placing them in view but out of reach (e.g., on a shelf, in a clear tub). As a student makes a request for a toy, the teacher may expand the student's communication response using incidental teaching strategies (Hart & Risley, 1978). Another example involves placing edible reinforcers in a tightly sealed clear container (e.g., peanut butter jar) during instruction. Following instructional trials, the teacher presents the container and prompts the student to say, "Open." Subsequently, the teacher provides immediate access to the reinforcer. The placement of preferred items in naturalistic contexts plays a vital role in the development of a spontaneous and generalized communication repertoire.

Antecedent Prompts and Visual Supports

Antecedent prompts and visual supports have been used to increase student success and independence across a wide range of skills. Antecedent prompting involves the manipulation of antecedent stimuli to increase student performance (Browder, Spooner, & Mims, 2011). For example, a teacher may present a pictured sequence of a chained task or a brief video depicting a desired response prior to asking the student to complete the task. Teachers should place antecedent prompts in critical areas to facilitate independence. Ultimately, these prompts should be faded.

Similarly, visual supports are used to help students understand what is expected of them. Visual supports can take many forms including calendars, activity schedules, cue cards, or the physical arrangement of materials. For example, a teacher may place three activities on a shelf in the order in which they are to be completed or affix a symbol on the bathroom door to remind students to wash their hands. Visual supports are not always faded and are often shaped to resemble supports used by persons without disabilities. A student may first learn to use a large picture schedule, but over time pictures are faded and the student carries a school agenda used by same-age peers without disabilities.

For most students, just placing a visual support within their instructional environment may not be sufficient. Teachers should select instructional strategies that will be used to teach students to use the supports. Several researchers have used graduated guidance to teach students to follow a schedule (Morrison, Sainato, Benchaaban, & Endo, 2002; Spriggs, Gast, & Ayres, 2007). For instance, Bryan and Gast (2000) used graduated guidance and a picture schedule to promote independent transitions across instructional activities. Following the presentation of a page of a photo album containing a picture depicting an activity to complete, the teacher manually prompted each student to complete the tasks. Once the students could follow the steps in the schedule, the physical prompts were faded. Visual supports may also be used to help students with ASD understand the passage of time. Teachers may use timers to indicate how long a student must engage in task, when a transition is to occur, or when reinforcement is available. Several types of timers are available including Time Timers (http://www.timetimer.com/), sand timers, and traditional egg timers. Another way to demonstrate the passing of time is by indicating progression through a daily or minischedule. Initially, teachers may mediate this process by pointing to scheduled items or by removing completed scheduled items. Gradually, teachers should instruct students how to monitor their own progress through a schedule.

Temporal Structure of Classroom Activities

The temporal structure of classroom activities also can play a vital role in student success. First, teachers must consider the length of instructional activities. These decisions should be individualized for each student but are often related to a student's skill repertoire and ability to work for a delayed reinforcement (Heflin & Alaimo, 2007). A student who loses motivation without frequent reinforcement may require shorter periods of instruction that involve continual opportunities to respond and be reinforced. Though it may be tempting for teachers to determine the length of an activity based on the amount of content to cover, they first should establish a length of time in which the student can respond success-fully and then gradually increase the duration of activity. This by no means suggests that students receive less time engaged in instruction, but that teachers intersperse brief instructional sessions between short intervals of preferred activities.

The strategy of interspersing preferred and nonpreferred activities to increase student engagement is firmly rooted in the research literature (e.g., Iwata & Micheal, 1994;

Premack, 1959) and can be easily implemented in classroom contexts. These strategies may be applied differently for students with dissimilar skill repertoires. For example, a teacher might consider arranging a high school student's schedule so that his favorite classes are 2nd, 4th, and 6th periods. Another teacher might intersperse 2 minutes of access to a computer game following 5 minutes of discrete trial training. Again, the amount of time between preferred activities will differ across students, but in general teachers should start where the student is successful and gradually make adjustments from that point.

Instructional Arrangement

Finally, it is important to consider the type of instructional arrangement that will be most effective during instruction. Collins, Gast, Ault, and Wolery (1991) suggested four types of arrangements frequently used during instruction: (a) one-to-one (1:1), (b) tandem, (c) small group, and (d) large group. Teachers should plan to provide instruction in various formats throughout the day. Students with limited skill repertoires may require 1:1 instructional arrangements to acquire skills more rapidly, especially if they have difficulty waiting for their turn to respond. During 1:1 instruction, teachers can deliver large numbers of trials and can closely monitor every element of instruction.

Group instructional formats may be challenging for some students with ASD. These formats may require students to wait while the teacher provides feedback to specific students, respond to peer interactions, and work for less frequent reinforcement. Collins and colleagues (1991) described the tandem format for transitioning students from 1:1 arrangements to group instruction. When using a tandem arrangement, a teacher works with a student in a 1:1 format alongside another teacher who is working with a small group of peers. Gradually, the student receives instructional trials in the small group format and the 1:1 support is faded.

Small group instruction provides a bridge from the intensive 1:1 instruction to the more naturalistic large group instruction that occurs in most general education classrooms. When using small group instruction, teachers can closely monitor student responses, deliver systematic instruction, and maintain high rates of reinforcement. Teachers can increase student engagement and can reduce wait time by using active responding strategies. These strategies involve having all students orally respond at once (i.e., chorale responding) or by having students simultaneously indicate their answer by writing on a dry erase/chalk board or by holding up a card with the correct answer on it (i.e., response cards; Horn, 2010). The success of any size instructional group lies in the effectiveness and efficiency of the teacher. In other words, the teacher must apply evidence-based instructional practices but also maintain a pace of instruction that ensures maximum opportunities for the student to respond and to access high rates of reinforcement.

Finally, teachers should plan supports for students in large group instructional contexts. The ability to acquire new skills in a large group setting is critical in maintaining access to general education classes and the content rich environments therein. Teachers should explicitly teach skills that are necessary to be successful during large group instruction (e.g., hand raising, attending to a speaker from a distance, tracking instructional stimuli). It is important to assess students frequently, as their difficulties attending to and comprehending in large group formats may be subtle. One additional consideration that should be made in general education classrooms is the placement and positioning of instructional support staff (i.e., paraprofessionals, related service staff). All efforts should be made to position support personnel in ways that do not impede access to the instruction delivered by the general education teacher or reduce interaction with students' natural peer supports.

Final Words

In conclusion, the careful arrangement of the educational environment can have a powerful impact on student performance. This arrangement is critical for students with ASD, in that many find their school experience to be wrought with challenges (Carrington & Graham, 2001; Simpson, Boer-Ott, & Smith-Myles, 2003). Fortunately, teachers have the power to design welcoming classrooms perceived by students with ASD to be safe, predictable, and highly reinforcing. Hopefully, the simple environmental arrangement strategies described in this chapter will serve as a good place to start.

References

Browder, D. M., Spooner, F. E., & Mims, P. (2011). Evidence-based practices. In D. M. Browder & F. Spooner (Eds.), *Teaching students with moderate to severe disabilities* (pp. 92-124). New York, NY: Guilford Press.

Bryan, L. C., & Gast, D. L. (2000). Teaching on-task and on schedule behaviors to high-functioning children with autism via picture activity schedules. *Journal of Autism and Developmental Disorders, 30,* 553-567.

Carrington, S., & Graham, L. (2001). Perceptions of school by two teenage boys with Asperger syndrome and their mothers: A qualitative study. *Autism: The International Journal of Research or Practice, 5,* 37-48.

Collins, B. C., Gast, D. L., Ault, M. J., & Wolery, M. (1991). Small group instruction: Guidelines for teachers of students with moderate to severe handicaps. *Education and Training in Mental Retardation, 26,* 18-32.

Hart, B. M., & Risley, T. R. (1978). Promoting productive language through incidental teaching. *Education and Urban Society, 10,* 407-429.

Heflin, L. J., & Alaimo, D. F. (2007). *Students with autism spectrum disorders: Effective instructional practices.* Upper Saddle Creek, NJ: Pearson.

Heward, W. L. (2009). *Exceptional children: An introduction to special education.* Upper Saddle Creek, NJ: Pearson.

Horn, C. (2010). Response cards: An effective intervention for students with disabilities. *Education and Training in Autism and Developmental Disabilities, 45,* 116-123.

Iwata, B. A., & Micheal, J. L. (1994). Applied applications of theory and research on the nature of reinforcement. *Journal of Applied Behavior Analysis, 27,* 183-193.

Morrison, R. S., Sainato, D. M., Benchaaban, D., & Endo, S. (2002). Increasing play skills of children with autism using activity schedules and correspondence training. *Journal of Early Intervention, 25,* 58-72.

Perrin, C. J., Perrin, S. H., Hill, E. A., & DiNovi, K. (2008). Brief functional analysis and treatment of preschoolers. *Behavior Interventions, 23,* 87-95.

Premack, D. (1959). Towards empirical behavior laws: I. Positive reinforcement. *Psychological Review, 66,* 219-233.

Simpson, R. L., Boer-Ott, S. R., & Smith-Myles, B. (2003). Inclusion of learners with autism spectrum disorders. *Topics in Language Disorders, 23,* 116-133.

Spriggs, A. D., Gast, D. L., & Ayres, K. M. (2007). Using picture schedule activity books to increase on-schedule and on-task behaviors. *Education and Training in Developmental Disabilities, 42,* 209-223.

Assessment for Program Planning

Brenda Smith Myles, Amy Bixler Coffin, Jill Hudson,
Renee A. Lake, Barry Grossman, and Ruth Aspy

Thorough assessment across domains and settings provides the information multidisciplinary teams need to create comprehensive individualized programs for students with autism spectrum disorders (ASD). Traditionally, program-planning assessment has focused on academic, daily living, social/emotional/behavioral, recreation and leisure, sensory and motor, and communication skills. Although these areas are important, assessment should also focus on the areas that impact the learner with ASD: (a) specific characteristics of ASDs that must be addressed through direct instruction, (b) levels of supports needed to access curriculum, (c) strengths that can be used as a vehicle for instruction and motivation, (d) futures planning to establish long- and short-term goals, and (e) instructional strategies that are consistent with student needs. Designing and implementing a comprehensive program that contains the aforementioned elements increases the student's academic achievement (Mesibov, 2008). This chapter introduces methods that multidisciplinary teams can use as they assess students with ASD as part of the process of designing effective, comprehensive programs.

Traditional Assessment

In addition to having knowledge of the complexity of ASD, teams must also understand the myriad types of assessment that can be utilized to develop a program for the learner with ASD. Two types of assessment used in program planning assessment are curriculum-based assessments (CBA) and criterion-referenced tests (CRT). CBA are useful for program planning because they are derived from the school's curriculum. Some teams may use CRT in addition to or instead of CBA to determine student skill levels. CRT provides information both on skills the student has mastered and those the student has not mastered although they are not directly derived from the learner's school curriculum. Both types of assessment emphasize whether or not the student can perform a task.

In this chapter, two areas of academic assessment will be reviewed: literacy and mathematics. Many of the skills in literacy and mathematics should be assessed at both the recognition *and* the recall level because learners with ASD may be able to respond at one level but not the other. Recognition-level questions provide a response cue to the student and include such question formats as true/false, yes/no, matching, and multiple choice. At the recall level, the students are asked to answer questions without a prompt or cue. Questions that are open-ended fit this category; responses can be a one-word answer ("What is the capitol of Delaware?") or a longer reply ("What were the causes of the Civil War?"). As such, the recall-level question is considered a more advanced format. For a more comprehensive picture of the student's skills, an assessment team may want to assess the student in a manner that requires both verbal response *and* a written response as well as provide questions both in written and verbal formats (Hudson, Colson, & Braxdale, as cited in Myles & Simpson, 2003).

As a first step in comprehensive program planning for students with ASD, English language arts, mathematics, and reinforcer assessment are briefly described. In addition, a method for screening for social/communication skills in inclusive environments will be highlighted. Finally, two innovative models, the Ziggurat Model (Aspy & Grossman, 2011) and the Comprehensive Autism Planning System (CAPS; Henry & Myles, 2007), will be used where data are matched to evidence-based interventions and seamlessly distributed throughout the student's day.

English Language Arts

Literacy, an area identified under the category of English Language Arts of the National Standards, is a complex area whose primary goal is comprehension (Koppenhaver, 2010). The areas of writing, speaking, and listening are equally complex (Wolfe, Williamson, & Carnahan, 2010). Many students with ASD may have strong decoding skills, sight vocabulary skills, and rote memory skills (Jacobs & Watts-Taffe, 2010), but as students progress through school, these skills become less important as more emphasis is placed on higher level thinking skills (Allor, Mathes, Roberts, Jones, & Champlin, 2010; Carnahan, Musti-Rao, & Bailey, 2009). That is, students with ASD might do well when assessed in the "Key Ideas and Details" area of Reading (see College and Career Readiness Anchor Standards for Reading; National Governors Association Center for Best Practices & Council of Chief State School Officers, 2010), but experience challenges in learning and expressing what they know relative to (a) craft and structure, (b) integration of knowledge and ideas, and (c) comprehension of complex literature (National Council of Teachers of English, n.d.).

This requires that an experienced multidisciplinary team work together to ensure that skills are assessed across environments (e.g., social studies, science). These specialists should assess a variety of language skills relative to the curricular and related demands, such as the student's communicative intent, language complexity, vocabulary, grammar, ability to sequence, and fluency.

Mathematics

Overall, mathematics is considered a hierarchical subject. Therefore, if early skills are not established, students will not be able to master later skills (Banda, McAfee, Lee, & Kubina, 2007). Some areas addressed in the National Standards for Mathematics (National Council of Teachers of Mathematics, n.d.), such as the content areas of numbers and operations and measurement are often strengths for individuals with ASD. Others, including the process standards of problem solving, reasoning and proof, communication, connection, and representation may be more challenging because of associated abstractions. Thus, it is recommended that skills be assessed at the concrete, semi-concrete, and abstract levels in each of these areas. Identification of skills at the three aforementioned levels aids in programming because it specifically targets where instruction is needed. For example, a student who cannot complete word problems presented in written format (abstract) may be able to complete them when provided a calculator (semiconcrete) or may need tangible items to count (concrete).

Reinforcer Assessment

Reinforcement, by definition, follows behavior and increases the likelihood that the behavior will occur again. It is a necessary part of the education of all students, including students with ASD. If there is no reinforcement, there is no learning (Frost & Bondy, 2002). Reinforcers for students with ASD are often different than for other children and youth. Research clearly states that access to items and activities related to special interests are strong reinforcers and do not increase preoccupation with the interests (Winter-Messiers et al., 2007). Stereotypic behaviors can be equally as powerful (Charlop, Kurtz, & Casey, 1990). A number of reinforcer assessments exist for students with ASD who are able to speak, including the Preference Reinforcement Assessment (Touch Autism, 2011) and the Reinforcer Assessment Grid (Wright, 2002). For students with ASD who have limited or no verbal skills, the minireinforcer assessment procedure, outlined in Table 2-1, is effective (Mason & Egel, 1995).

Social/Communication Assessment: Screening for Skills That Promote Successful Inclusion

General education teachers revealed in a recent study that they believed their skills in managing students with ASD were strong, but the students were often unprepared to meet the demands of the classroom (Rosen, Rotheram-Fuller, & Mandell, 2011). What skills do students, including students with ASD, need to be successful in inclusive classrooms? These skills are not academic in nature but fall in the range of social, communication, and teacher-pleasing behaviors. Many of these skills are especially challenging for students with ASD. As such, it is important that these skills be assessed and taught. Table 2-2 provides a list of these skills with subskills that can be used as a screening measure for students in or entering inclusive settings (Myles, Aspy, & Grossman, in press). Items reflect research on teachers' perceptions of the behaviors required for successful inclusion (Kerr & Zigmond, 1986; Lane, Pierson, & Givner, 2003).

Table 2-1

Steps to Conducting a Reinforcer Preference Assessment for Students With ASD With Limited Verbal Skills

1. Start with a pool of items that may be reinforcing for the student. It is often easiest to observe the student to determine the sensory input she enjoys. For example if she seeks visual input, work with the OT to identify visually-based items that may serve as reinforcers. Identify 10 to 20 objects in this category.

2. Organize two containers: (a) one for items selected and (b) one for items not selected. If an object will not fit into a container, place a picture in the container.

3. While sitting with the student, show her two items and give the direction, "Pick one."

4. Provide adequate wait time for the student to select an item using her form of communication (e.g., visual orientation, reach, point, switch). Allow the student to interact with the item for a brief time period (i.e., 30 seconds using a visual/auditory timer to indicate start and end time).

5. Place items in the appropriate container (selected/not selected).

6. Continue the selection process until all items are presented to the student and placed in the proper container.

7. Place the container near the student's work area for reinforcement as appropriate.

Note. This can be done initially to identify a bank of reinforcers and then on a daily basis to identify items that are reinforcing for the student on that particular day. ASD = autism spectrum disorders; OT = occupational therapist.

Table 2-2

Student Behaviors That Facilitate Inclusion Success	
STUDENT NAME: _____ Indicate mastery level of each inclusion behavior. If behavior is not mastered or emerging, indicate the supports that are needed.	DATE: _____
INCLUSION BEHAVIORS	**NEEDS**
Complies with teacher commands	●——————————————————● Not mastered Emerging Mastered
Underlying Needs/Challenges ❑ Expresses strong need for routine or "sameness" ❑ Asks repetitive questions ❑ Interprets words or conversations literally/has difficulty understanding figurative language ❑ Displays poor problem-solving skills ❑ Exhibits rage reactions or "meltdowns"	**Instruction/Supports Needed**
Follows established classroom rules	●——————————————————● Not mastered Emerging Mastered
Underlying Needs/Challenges ❑ Has problems handling transition and change ❑ Has difficulty stopping a task before it is completed ❑ Displays poor problem-solving skills ❑ Displays typical activity level ❑ Exhibits rage reactions or "meltdowns"	**Instruction/Supports Needed**
Produces work corresponding with ability and skills level	●——————————————————● Not mastered Emerging Mastered
Underlying Needs/Challenges ❑ Displays poor problem-solving skills ❑ Has poor organizational skills ❑ Is easily distracted by unrelated details ❑ Displays weakness in reading comprehension with strong word recognition ❑ Knows many facts and details but has difficulty with abstract reasoning ❑ Recalls information consistently ❑ Has poor handwriting ❑ Writes slowly ❑ Has difficulty starting or completing actions	**Instruction/Supports Needed**

Table 2-2 *(continued)*

Student Behaviors That Facilitate Inclusion Success	
INCLUSION BEHAVIORS	**NEEDS**
Attends to and follows oral instructions given for assignments	●———————————————● Not mastered Emerging Mastered
Underlying Needs/Challenges ❏ Interprets words or conversations literally/has difficulty understanding figurative language ❏ Has problems handling transition and change ❏ Has difficulty following instruction ❏ Has difficulty understanding language with multiple meanings, humor, sarcasm, or synonyms ❏ Has attention problems ❏ Has difficulty starting or completing actions	**Instruction/Supports Needed**
Expresses anger appropriately	●———————————————● Not mastered Emerging Mastered
Underlying Needs/Challenges ❏ Has difficulty expressing thoughts and feelings ❏ Is easily stressed – worries obsessively ❏ Exhibits rage reactions or "meltdowns"	**Instruction/Supports Needed**
Interacts with peers without becoming hostile and angry	●———————————————● Not mastered Emerging Mastered
Underlying Needs/Challenges ❏ Has difficulty recognizing the feelings and thoughts of others ❏ Uses poor eye contact ❏ Has difficulty maintaining personal space ❏ Lacks tact or appears rude ❏ Has difficulty making or keeping friends ❏ Has difficulty joining an activity ❏ Has difficulty understanding others' nonverbal communication ❏ Has difficulty understanding jokes ❏ Has difficulty talking about others' interests ❏ Exhibits rage reactions or "meltdowns" ❏ Has difficulty tolerating mistakes	**Instruction/Supports Needed**

Table 2-2 *(continued)*

Student Behaviors That Facilitate Inclusion Success	
INCLUSION BEHAVIORS	**NEEDS**
Regulates behavior in non-classroom settings	Not mastered Emerging Mastered
Underlying Needs/Challenges ❑ Has difficulty understanding the connection between behavior and resulting consequences ❑ Exhibits rage reactions or "meltdowns" ❑ Is easily stressed – worries obsessively ❑ Has low frustration tolerance ❑ Has difficulty tolerating mistakes	**Instruction/Supports Needed**
Responds appropriately to peer pressure pertaining to classroom rules	Not mastered Emerging Mastered
Underlying Needs/Challenges ❑ Exhibits rage reactions or "meltdowns" ❑ Has difficulty understanding jokes ❑ Has difficulty understanding language with multiple meanings, humor, sarcasm, or synonyms	**Instruction/Supports Needed**
Requests assistance in an appropriate manner when needed	Not mastered Emerging Mastered
Underlying Needs/Challenges ❑ Has difficulty applying learned skills in new settings ❑ Has difficulty tolerating mistakes ❑ Has difficulty managing stress and/or anxiety	**Instruction/Supports Needed**

Note. From "Introduction to Assessment: Screening and Evaluation," by B. S. Myles, R. Aspy, and B. G. Grossman, in press. In B. G. Grossman, R. Aspy, & B. S. Myles (Eds.). *Transdisciplinary evaluation of autism spectrum disorders: From diagnosis through program planning.* Shawnee Mission, KS: AAPC. Copyright in press by AAPC. Reprinted with permission.

Customized Program Planning

The second step in program planning assessment consists of matching learner characteristics, both strengths and challenges, to interventions, and then embedding the interventions throughout the student's day. Two models, the Ziggurat Model (Aspy & Grossman, 2008) and the CAPS (Henry & Myles, 2007), provide practitioners with a process and framework for linking learner characteristics to evidence-based interventions. The Ziggurat Model begins with an assessment of the specific characteristics of the student's underlying autism using the Underlying Characteristics Checklist (UCC)—of which there are three versions: UCC-HF (high functioning), UCC-CL (classic), and UCC-EI (early intervention)—and the Individual Strengths and Skills Inventory (ISSI). All contain items in the following areas: (a) social differences, (b) restrictive patterns of behaviors/interests/activities, (c) communication differences, (d) sensory differences, (e) cognitive differences, (f) motor differences, (g) emotional vulnerability, and (h) known medical/biological factors. The team then collaboratively identifies long- and short-term goals for the student using the Global Intervention Plan. From this process, the team prioritizes items from the UCC to develop an intervention plan using the Intervention Ziggurat (IZ). The IZ is based on interventions in five areas: (a) Sensory Differences and Biological Needs, (b) Reinforcement, (c) Structure and Visual/Tactile Supports, (d) Task Demands, and (e) Skills to Teach because learners with ASD typically need multiple interventions across these five areas to successfully navigate the curriculum. Interventions at each level are then chosen to match specific underlying characteristics (identified on the UCC). This step ensures that "the ASD" in each individual is addressed using meaningful, positive interventions. The final step occurs when team members embed the interventions determined through use of the Ziggurat Model throughout the student's day using the CAPS. Figure 2-1 outlines this process.

Conclusion

Assessment for program planning is a complex process intended to culminate in a highly individualized set of interventions. Once the initial assessment has been completed to identify the student's (a) school-related skills and (b) strengths and challenges, this information is utilized to develop interventions matched specifically to the student's strengths and needs. Finally, interventions are embedded into the student's daily schedule. A strong assessment for the purposes of planning a program is the initial step in providing the student with ASD an opportunity to meet his/her potential.

Figure 2-1

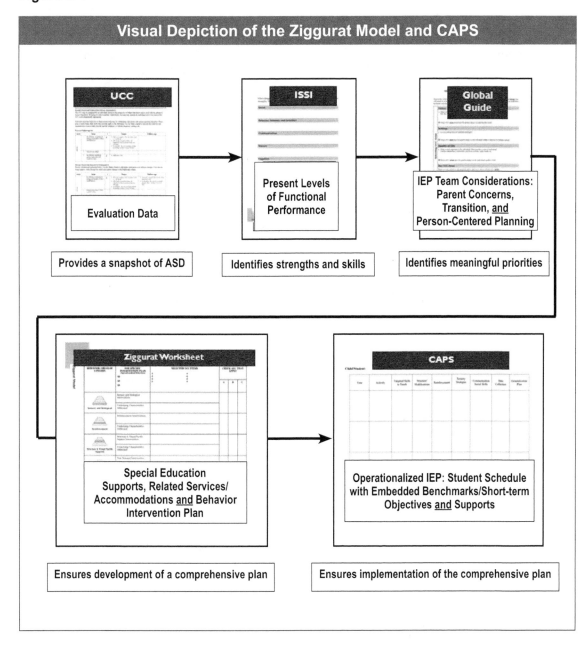

Visual Depiction of the Ziggurat Model and CAPS

UCC — Evaluation Data — Provides a snapshot of ASD

ISSI — Present Levels of Functional Performance — Identifies strengths and skills

Global Guide — IEP Team Considerations: Parent Concerns, Transition, and Person-Centered Planning — Identifies meaningful priorities

Ziggurat Worksheet — Special Education Supports, Related Services/ Accommodations and Behavior Intervention Plan — Ensures development of a comprehensive plan

CAPS — Operationalized IEP: Student Schedule with Embedded Benchmarks/Short-term Objectives and Supports — Ensures implementation of the comprehensive plan

Note. From "Introduction to Assessment: Screening and Evaluation," by B. S. Myles, R. Aspy, and B. G. Grossman, in press. In B. G. Grossman, R. Aspy, & B. S. Myles (Eds.). *Transdisciplinary evaluation of autism spectrum disorders: From diagnosis through program planning*. Shawnee Mission, KS: AAPC. Copyright in press by AAPC. Reprinted with permission.

References

Allor, J. H., Mathes, P. G., Roberts, J. K., Jones, F. G., & Champlin, T. M. (2010). Teaching students with moderate intellectual disabilities to read: An experimental examination of a comprehensive reading intervention. *Education and Training in Autism and Developmental Disabilities, 45,* 3-22.

Aspy, R., & Grossman, B. G. (2011). *Designing comprehensive interventions for individuals with high-functioning autism and Asperger Syndrome: The Ziggurat Model* (2nd ed.). Shawnee Mission, KS: AAPC.

Banda, D. R., McAfee, J. K., Lee, D. L., & Kubina, R. M. (2007). Math preference and mastery relationship in middle school students with autism spectrum disorders. *Journal of Behavioral Education, 16,* 207-223.

Carnahan, C., Musti-Rao, S., & Bailey, J. (2009). Promoting active engagement in small group learning experiences for students with autism and significant learning needs. *Education and Treatment of Children, 32,* 37-61.

Charlop, M. H., Kurtz, P. F., & Casey, F. G. (1990). Using aberrant behaviors as reinforcers for autistic children. *Journal of Applied Behavior Analysis, 23,* 163-181.

Frost, L., & Bondy, A. (2002). *The Picture Exchange Communication System training manual.* Newark, DE: Pyramid Educational Products.

Henry, S. A., & Myles, B. S. (2007). *The Comprehensive Autism Planning Systems (CAPS) for individuals with Asperger Syndrome, autism and related disabilities: Integrating best practices throughout the student's day.* Shawnee Mission, KS: AAPC.

Jacobs, J., & Watts-Taffe, S. (2010). Vocabulary. In C. Carnahan & P. Williamson (Eds.), *Quality literacy instruction for students with autism spectrum disorders* (pp. 321-354). Shawnee Mission, KS: AAPC.

Kerr, M. M., & Zigmond, N. (1986). What do high school teachers want? A study of expectations and standards. *Education and Treatment of Children, 9,* 239–249.

Koppenhaver, D. (2010). Reading comprehensive. In C. Carnahan & P. Williamson (Eds.), *Quality literacy instruction for students with autism spectrum disorders* (pp. 355-386). Shawnee Mission, KS: AAPC.

Lane, K. L., Pierson, M. R., & Givner, C. C. (2003). Teacher expectations of student behavior: Which skills do elementary and secondary teachers deem necessary for success in the classroom? *Education and Treatment of Children, 26,* 413–418.

Mason, S. A., & Egel, A. L. (1995). What does Amy like? Using a mini-reinforcer assessment to increase student participation in instructional activities. *TEACHING Exceptional Children, 28*(1), 42-45.

Mesibov, G. (2008). Foreword. In B. G. Grossman & R. Aspy (Eds.), *Designing comprehensive interventions for individuals with high-functioning autism and Asperger Syndrome: The Ziggurat Model* (pp. xiii-xiv). Shawnee Mission, KS: AAPC.

Myles, B. S., Aspy, R., & Grossman, B. G. (in press). Introduction to assessment: Screening and evaluation. In B. G. Grossman, R. Aspy, & B. S. Myles. (Eds.), *Transdisciplinary evaluation of autism spectrum disorders: From diagnosis through program planning.* Shawnee Mission, KS: AAPC.

Myles, B. S., & Simpson, R. L. (2003). *Asperger Syndrome: A guide for educators and parents* (2nd ed.). Austin, TX: Pro-Ed.

National Council of Teachers of Teachers of English. (n.d.). *English language arts standards anchor standards >> college and career readiness anchor standards for reading.* Retrieved from http://www.corestandards.org/the-standards/english-language-arts-standards/anchor-standards/college-and-career-readiness-anchor-standards-for-reading

National Council of Teachers of Mathematics. (n.d.). *Executive summary: Principles and standards for school mathematics.* Retrieved from http://www.nctm.org/uploadedFiles/Math_Standards/12752_exec_pssm.pdf

National Governors Association Center for Best Practices & Council of Chief State School Officers. (2010). *Common Core State Standards Initiative, College and Career Readiness Anchor Standards for Reading.* Retrieved from http://www.corestandards.org/the-standards/english-language-arts-standards/anchor-standards/college-and-career-readiness-anchor-standards-for-reading/

Rosen, P., Rotheram-Fuller, E., & Mandell, D. S. (2011, May 12-14). *General education teachers' perceptions of inclusion for children with autism.* Proceedings of the International Society for Autism Research. Retrieved from http://imfar.confex.com/imfar/2011/webprogram/start.html

Touch Autism. (Producer). (2011, May). *Preference and Reinforcer Assessment Lite.* Retrieved from http://itunes.apple.com/us/app/preference-reinforcer-assessment/id440300890?mt=8&ign-mpt=uo%3D2

Winter-Messiers, M. A., Herr, C. M., Wood, C. E., Brooks, A. P., Gates, M. M.; Houston, T. L., & Tingstad, K. I. (2007). How far can Brian ride the Daylight 4449 Express? A strength-based model of Asperger syndrome based on special interest areas. *Focus on Autism and Other Developmental Disabilities, 22,* 67-79.

Wolfe, J., Williamson, P., & Carnahan, C. (2010). Writing instruction. In C. Carnahan & P. Williamson (Eds.), *Quality literacy instruction for students with autism spectrum disorders* (pp. 387-408). Shawnee Mission, KS: AAPC.

Wright, J. (2002). *Reinforcer Assessment Grid.* Retrieved from http://www.jimwrightonline.com/pdfdocs/rftassessment1.pdf

Progress Monitoring

Barbara A. Wilson

Overall, the use of progress monitoring results in more efficient and appropriately targeted instructional techniques and goals, which together, move all students to faster attainment of important state standards of achievement. (National Center on Student Progress Monitoring, n.d., What Are the Benefits of Progress Monitoring section, para 2)

Student progress data are increasingly emphasized in education, as most states now conduct routine standardized assessments of all students in addition to the specific testing requirements of federal education laws. Primarily summative in nature, these assessments typically report on the effectiveness of learning postinstruction and consequently provide limited information on student progress as instruction is being implemented. Progress monitoring is a system of data collection and analysis that provides on-going information regarding student learning and instructional effectiveness. It also addresses a number of needs relevant to educating students with autism spectrum disorders (ASD) and provides information on student progress throughout instruction so that instruction can be modified to better meet the unique learning needs of the student. The data compiled through progress monitoring can also be used to meet federal requirements that eligible students' individualized education programs (IEPs) contain measurable goals with progress reported periodically throughout the year (Yell, 2006). Progress monitoring is a flexible system that easily lends itself to measuring progress on the variety of academic, communication, self-help, and behavioral goals that are often identified for students with ASD.

Overview of Progress Monitoring and Its Benefits

According to the National Center on Student Progress Monitoring (n.d.), progress monitoring utilizes brief assessments, typically delivered weekly to monthly, to measure student progress on a specific skill across time. By comparing the results of these student assessments to anticipated achievement rates (e.g., IEP goal annual mastery criteria, short-term benchmarks, or state standards), teachers can determine if their instructional strategies are resulting in adequate student progress and, in the event that progress is not satisfactory, modify that instruction. Consider, for example, Tyree, a second-grade student with an IEP goal that states, "When greeted by peers and adults, Tyree will respond with 'hello'(using his Dynavox) during 9/10 daily opportunities by the end of the school year." Although a plan for teaching and reinforcing this skill was developed and implemented, Tyree's teacher was only able to determine the effectiveness of her instruction by looking at the data she collected on Tyree's use of the skill across several weeks and comparing it to the projected rates he would need to meet his annual goal. In this example, Tyree's teacher noticed (by reviewing several weeks of data on the number of times each day that Tyree responded to greetings) that Tyree was not making adequate progress on this skill. Based on this information, she modified her teaching and reinforcement of this skill.

The National Center on Progress Monitoring (n.d.) identifies a number of benefits for both students and teachers when progress monitoring is consistently and correctly utilized, including increased academic growth, fewer referrals for special education services, and increased learning expectations. Teachers experience better communication with parents regarding their students' progress and are able to make more knowledgeable decisions regarding instructional methods and strategies. In short, progress monitoring constitutes a simple and effective method for assessing teaching and learning.

Measurable Goals: A Basic Requirement for Progress Monitoring

Progress monitoring begins with the identification of measurable annual goals. Whether these goals are from the student's IEP or are drawn from state or local educational standards, at a minimum they need to contain a statement of the conditions under which the behavior will be performed, the observable and measurable behavior the student will be expected to perform, and specific achievement criteria to be met (Gibb & Dychess, 2007). Tyree's goal is an example of a complete and measurable goal as it contains all of the critical elements: When greeted by peers and adults (conditions), Tyree will respond with "hello" (using his Dynavox; observable and measurable behavior) during 9/10 daily opportunities by the end of the school year (specific achievement criteria). Clearly written goals will guide both instruction and the development of a data collection system.

Given the variety of academic, life skills and behavioral needs frequently experienced by students with ASD, teachers should carefully consider the variety of measurement options available when writing measurable goals to ensure they reflect the desired yearly outcome. A description of measurement metrics and examples of their use are shown in Table 3-1.

Table 3-1		
Data Types and Uses		
Data Type	**Use When Goal Is to**	**Examples**
Accuracy	Teach the skill to be used correctly with no time limit	• Compute all multiplication facts 1-12 with 90% accuracy • Independently complete all steps required to purchase drink from vending machine (100% accuracy)
Frequency	Increase or decrease the number of times a student engages in a target behavior across a specific time period	• Appropriately greet peers seven times each school day • Decrease instances of "calling out" to no more than two per school day
Fluency	Increase the rate of skill performance over a specific amount of time (often used for correct per minute academic skills)	• Increase reading rate of third grade reading material to 100 words correct per minute • Complete 50 basic math facts in 2 minutes
Duration	Increase or decrease the total amount of time a student engages in a specific behavior	• Increase the time spent in sustained silent reading to 15 minutes • Decrease the amount of time engaged in self-stimulatory behaviors to no more than 2 minutes per day
Latency	Decrease the amount of time between a stimulus and the expected response	• Will move toward the building exit within 10 seconds of hearing the fire alarm • Will respond via his Dynavox to peer greetings within 10 seconds

Data Collection and Graphing

With the observable goal and mastery criteria for instruction clearly identified, the teacher must consider when and how he/she will collect raw data on the student's performance of the skill. There are many Internet resources available to teachers for collecting data on the academic skills of reading, mathematics, written expression, and spelling (see Internet Resources list at the end of this chapter). However, functional skills, vocational skills, or skills focusing on behavior change may be so individualized that the teacher must design his/her own data sheet. In these cases, the nature of the goal will readily suggest the type of data that should be collected. Consider the goal "When transitioning outdoors, Stella will independently put on her coat 3/3 opportunities by January 20." To collect data on this goal, the teacher needs to individualize the steps (by conducting a detailed task analysis) of the data sheet to reflect the unique demands of the task, including Stella's preferred handedness, the type of coat closures, and so forth. Once a task analysis of this skill has been completed, the teacher can use the steps to design a data sheet to record Stella's performance on each step of the task.

The task analysis developed for Stella with the data collected during the first 6 weeks of instruction is depicted in Table 3-2. Although this example shows a skill that requires a series of specific steps to complete, there are other skills that may not lend themselves to a task analytic format, including some academic or communication skills. For example, Tyree's goal of "will respond to peer and adult greetings 9/10 daily opportunities" will lend itself to a data sheet that identifies the 10 opportunities rather than a task analysis format.

One of the strengths of progress monitoring is the use of a visual display to show student progress across time. Visual representation removes the need to calculate an average performance from raw data and simplifies instructional decision making. By graphing the raw data obtained across several weeks and comparing these to the anticipated progress required to meet the short-term or annual goal, it is easy to determine whether instruction is effective or requires modification.

Setting up a graph can be done through any one of several online services or by using a graphing program such as Excel. However, it is easy to make and maintain using graph paper. To begin, consider the range of scores the student is likely to exhibit on the specific skill. This range should be listed on the vertical axis of the graph. The horizontal axis represents the time range during which you anticipate that the student will be working on the skill and is typically divided into equal intervals representing days or weeks. Using Stella's skill of independently putting on her coat, the range of scores she could obtain would be from 0 (with no independent steps completed) to 10 (independence on all steps of the task). These scores become the range on the vertical axis of the graph. Stella's

Table 3-2

Putting On Coat Task Analysis With Data							
Steps of Task Analysis	**Nov. 9**	**Nov. 16**	**Nov. 23**	**Nov. 30**	**Dec. 5**	**Dec. 12**	**Dec. 19**
1. Pick up coat by collar with left hand with inside of coat facing away from body	P	P	P	I	I	I	I
2. Swing coat over shoulders	P	P	P	P	P	P	P
3. Reach right hand over shoulder	P	P	P	P	P	P	P
4. Locate right sleeve with right hand and push hand into sleeve	P	P	P	P	P	P	P
5. Locate left sleeve with left hand and push hand into sleeve	P	I	P	I	P	P	P
6. Adjust shoulders	P	P	P	P	I	I	I
7. Align buttons	P	P	P	P	P	I	I
8. Button lower button	P	P	I	P	P	P	P
9. Button middle button	P	P	P	I	I	I	I
10. Button top button	I	I	I	I	I	I	I
Total Independent Steps	1	2	2	4	4	5	5

Note: I = Independent; P = Physically Assisted.

teacher determined that Stella should be able to master the skill within 10 weeks, and that she would teach the skill daily but take data for graphing purposes once each week. Consequently, the horizontal axis on Stella's graph was divided into 10 weekly intervals.

With the graph completed, one more step is needed to determine whether the student is progressing adequately toward goal mastery; drawing in the aimline. The aimline represents the rate of skill growth needed for the student to meet the goal by the stated mastery date. Determining aimlines may require some math, but the result is a clear line on the graph that shows the level of skill mastery that is required for the student to master their goal. If your graph paper shows the entire time period that you will be working on the skill, it is simple to draw in your aimline. Begin by marking the preinstruction or current rate of the skill on the graph on the first week of instruction (typically available in the student's IEP or from baseline data in the skill collected prior to beginning instruction) and then mark the performance goal on the last week of instruction. Join the two marks with a straight line.

The graph and aimline developed for Stella are in Figure 3-1. Note that the aimline begins at the point of Stella's current level of performance. (Stella cannot complete any of the steps of the task analysis independently.) The aimline ends at the last instructional week, at the point where her teacher anticipates that she will independently complete all steps of the task analysis. The aimline represents the weekly performance Stella will need in order to meet her goal within the 10-week time frame determined by her teacher.

If you are graphing across several sheets (as may be the case if you are recording data for an annual goal) the mathematics required for determining aimlines is slightly more involved but still relatively straightforward. The goal "When given an oral reading probe of middle fourth grade reading material, Sven will increase his rate of words correct per minute to 100 words correct per minute by the end of the school year" will be used to illustrate how to develop an aimline across several graphs for this skill. Begin by determining the student's rate at the beginning of the graphing period. In this example, Sven was reading 37 words correct per minute (his average when given several probes of middle fourth grade material during the first week of school in September). This figure, when subtracted from the annual goal rate, gives the growth required to meet the annual goal (100 - 37 = 63). In this example, Sven needs to "grow" by 63 correct words per minute to meet his annual goal. The next step is to divide this figure by the amount of time the student has to meet this goal. For short-term goals, you will want to calculate the number of weeks that the student will be working on the goal. For annual goals, you will want to divide by the number of months in the school year. In Sven's case, his goal was written for a nine month school year, so his annual "growth" figure was divided by the number of months he has to work on the goal, or 9 (63/9 = 7). Using this figure, we know that Sven needs to increase his rate of words correct per minute by seven each month of the school year to meet his annual goal.

Figure 3-1

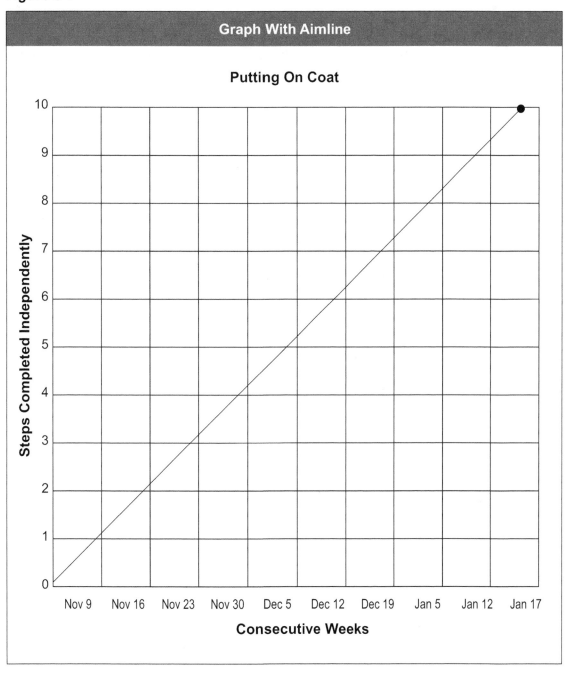

With Sven's current (beginning of goal) rate and monthly required growth calculated, it is simple to determine Sven's required reading rate for any month, and from there to draw the aimline. In this case, Sven's school year began the first week of September, and Sven had a reading rate of 37 words correct per minute. To be on target for meeting his annual goal, Sven needs to increase his rate of reading by seven words correct each month, so his required rate for the first week of October is his baseline rate (37) plus his required monthly growth (7), or 44. His rate for the first week of November would reflect his October rate (44) plus his monthly required growth (7), or 51. In this way, his required rates for any month can be determined and graphed as an aimline. Using these figures, graphs for any period of time across a school year can be developed to reflect the aimline.

Tracking Student Progress and Making Data-Based Decisions

With the data sheet and graph developed, data can be collected and analyzed for decision making purposes. Browder (2001) noted the importance of having a set of rules for evaluating data and making instructional decisions. Although many sets of rules have been developed (Hintze & Marcotte, 2010), the three-point decision rule is simple to implement and provides a set of guidelines for evaluating data. As described by Wright (n.d.), data are evaluated on an ongoing schedule using *the three most recent data points*. In this way, each time a new data point is recorded on the graph, decisions about the effectiveness of the current instructional plan can be made. The rules are simple:

1. If the last three data points are below the aimline, change in intervention is required.
2. If the last three data points are around the aimline, no change is required.
3. If the last three data points are above the aimline, the aimline should be made more challenging (or, if mastery criteria have been met, additional learning goals developed).

By applying these rules to the data collected for Stella (see Figure 3-2), her teacher made a series of weekly decisions beginning on November 23, the first date in which there were three data points. As Stella's teacher entered the data in the graph, she looked at the data for November 9, 16, and 23, and noted that the data were around the aimline—indicating that no change in instruction was needed. Stella's progress indicated that she was on target for mastering the skill. The next week she reviewed the most recent three data points (November 16, 23, 30) and again noted that they were around the aimline. She continued with the weekly review of data, noting that no change in intervention was needed until the week of December 19, when Stella's graph showed three consecutive points below the aimline. Stella's teacher recognized that a change in instruction was required, as Stella was no longer on target for mastering putting on her coat by the mastery date. Stella's teacher considered many aspects of her teaching plan for Stella, including the frequency of teaching, methods and setting, among others (McLane, n.d.) before selecting the modification that she believed would best improve Stella's learning.

Figure 3-2

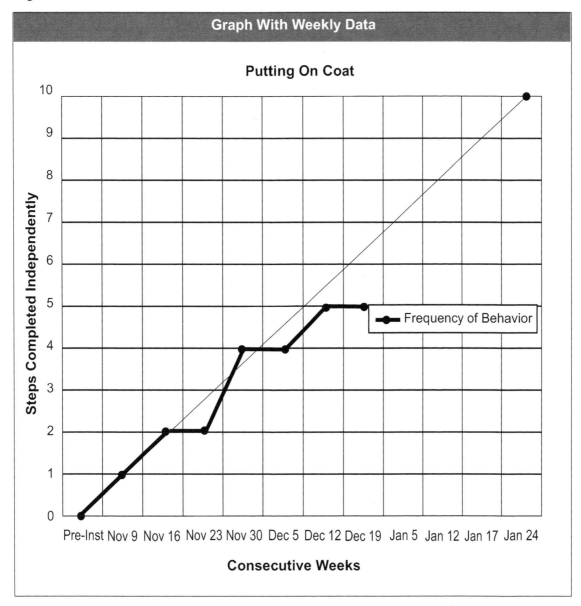

Graph With Weekly Data

Putting On Coat

Steps Completed Independently

Frequency of Behavior

Pre-Inst Nov 9 Nov 16 Nov 23 Nov 30 Dec 5 Dec 12 Dec 19 Jan 5 Jan 12 Jan 17 Jan 24

Consecutive Weeks

Conclusion

To ensure that students are making adequate progress toward meeting their annual goals, teachers need a strategy for determining the effectiveness of their instruction on student progress. Progress monitoring is a simple and time-efficient method for assessing student progress throughout the school year. By utilizing periodic probes of student performance, graphs with aimlines, and decision rules, teachers can easily determine when their instruction is effective or when teaching strategies require change, thereby improving student learning.

References

Browder, D. M. (2001). *Curriculum and assessment for students with moderate and severe disabilities.* New York, NY: Guilford Press.

Gibb, G. S., & Dychess, T. T. (2007). *Guide to writing quality individualized education programs* (2nd ed.). Boston, MA: Pearson Education.

Hintze, J. M., & Marcotte, A. M. (2010). Student assessment and data-based decision making. In T. A. Glover & S. Vaughn (Eds.), *The promise of response to intervention: Evaluating current science and practice* (pp. 57-77). New York, NY: Guilford Press.

McLane, K. (n.d.). Student progress monitoring: What this means for your child. Retrieved from http://www.osepideasthatwork.org/parentkit/studentprog.asp

National Center on Student Progress Monitoring (n.d.). Common questions for progress monitoring. Retrieved from http://www.studentprogress.org/progresmon.asp

Wright, J. (n.d.). Curriculum-based measurement: A manual for teachers. Retrieved from http://www.jimwrightonline.com/pdfdocs/cbaManual.pdf

Yell, M. L. (2006). *The law and special education* (2nd ed.). Upper Saddle River, NJ: Merrill/Prentice Hall.

Internet Resources

http://www.interventioncentral.com/
The CBM Warehouse section of this site contains detailed directions for conducting academic probes, graphing helps, and preprinted probe materials.

http://www.easycbm.com/
This site provides materials, graphing, and reports for academic assessments for individual students or groups.

https://dibels.uoregon.edu/
Resources for academic skills assessment in reading and math. Also offers a data system for a fee.

Section II
Effective Instructional Strategies

Systematic Instruction

Kara Hume

One goal of educators is to increase student engagement and active participation in classroom activities, using specific materials, and during interactions with peers and staff across the school day. Research has indicated that engaged behavior in students with disabilities is the single best predictor of academic gains (Bulgren & Carta, 1993). Similarly, the amount of time a student with autism spectrum disorders (ASD) is actively engaged in or attending to activities and interactions has been cited as one of the best predictors of student outcome (Iovannone, Dunlap, Huber, & Kincaid, 2003). However, characteristics related to a student's ASD, such as difficulty planning and organizing, limited ability to ignore competing information in the classroom, and challenges making connections between content/ideas (Hill, 2004), often make active engagement in the school setting difficult. If active engagement is going to be achieved with students with ASD, systematic instruction must be implemented to meet the needs of these students. Careful planning about how information will be presented and how students will respond is required to ensure the greatest likelihood that engagement will occur.

What Is Systematic Instruction?

Iovannone et al. (2003) defined systematic instruction for students with ASD as "planning for instruction by. . .carefully outlining instructional procedures, evaluating the effectiveness of the teaching procedures, and adjusting instruction based on data. . ." (p. 157). Essentially, educators should specifically plan *how to* provide instruction based on the needs and characteristics of their students with ASD while planning for high levels of engagement (Iovannone et al., 2003).

What Strategies Are Used and How Are They Implemented?

The instructional strategies used to facilitate systematic instruction discussed in this chapter are included for several reasons. First, there is an evidence base that supports their usage with students on the autism spectrum. In 2007, the Office of Special Education Programs in the U.S. Department of Education funded the National Professional Development Center on Autism Spectrum Disorders (NPDC) to promote the use of Evidence-Based Practices (EBP) in programs for infants, children, and youth with ASD and their families. The NPDC has identified 24 instructional strategies that meet criteria to be deemed evidence-based practices (see Odom, Collet-Klinenberg, Rogers, & Hatton, 2010, for information about how research was reviewed and rated). All of the strategies discussed in this chapter meet the stringent requirements of the NPDC. Second, these strategies are easily applicable in a classroom setting with one or more students with ASD. And last, they are practices that, though intended primarily for students with ASD, can benefit a broad range of students, including those with attention, organization, and processing issues. In addition to being identified as EBPs by NPDC, each of the strategies discussed in this chapter is based on the science of Applied Behavior Analysis (ABA). ABA is the use of behavioral techniques to teach new skills or modify one's behavior (for further description of ABA and its application to students with ASD, see Boutot & Hume, 2010).

Task Analysis

Breaking complex behavior into its component parts is called task analysis (Alberto & Troutman, 2006). It is the foundation of many instructional strategies for students with ASD and can be used to break skills down into manageable pieces. Skills, such as identifying the title of a book, can be parsed into many steps and taught in a number of phases. It is important to first identify what skills the student currently has, such as orienting the book properly and identifying the title page. Next, all components of the task should be listed in the order in which they are to be performed. For the skill, identifying the title of a book, these components may include recognizing the features of a title such as capitalization, placement on a page, and position relative to other text. Once each component step is taught and this skill is mastered it can be incorporated into a more complex task such as finding a specific title at the library, identifying the author of specific titles, or grouping books by designated genres based on titles. Conducting task analyses requires practice, but can be valuable when teaching students with ASD. Systematically identifying skills that students can already demonstrate and the steps needed for skills mastery will greatly reduce student failure and in turn increase engagement (Alberto & Troutman, 2006). To sharpen task analysis skills, select a simple task like brushing teeth and list its component parts in sequence. Then read the steps out loud to a partner while he/she does what you instruct. It will be quickly evident what steps you missed (e.g., if the partner is trying to put toothpaste on the brush with the cap still on) and your skills will improve over time (Hume, 2010). Additional information can be found in the Internet Resources section at the end of this chapter.

Discrete Trial Training

Discrete trial training (DTT) is likely one of the most widely researched and well-used instructional strategies for students with ASD. Typically conducted in a one-to-one setting in a distraction-free environment, DTT uses what is called a three-term contingency for instruction (Boutot & Hume, 2010; Smith, 2001). The three-term contingency includes some antecedent cue, or discriminative stimulus (S^D) provided by the teacher, followed by a behavioral response by the student (which in some cases may require teacher prompting to elicit), followed by a reinforcing consequence delivered by the teacher (Boutot & Hume, 2010). Table 4-1 provides a visual example of the three-term contingency (Boutot & Hume, 2010). Each learning opportunity utilizing this three-term contingency is referred to as a trial. Because it is used to teach skills that typically involve short, discrete behavioral responses (e.g., pointing to an item, answering a question), it is referred to as discrete trial training or discrete trial teaching.

Table 4-1		
Visual Example of the Three-Term Contingency		
Antecedent/Instructional Cue/S^D: Teacher asks child to "Show me blue"	Behavioral Response: Child touches blue cube	Reinforcing Consequence: Teacher gives student a high five

Prompting

Once the steps necessary to complete an activity are identified, teachers may then begin instructing students, often using a discrete trial format as described previously. Teachers often need to provide prompts to the students to encourage the correct behavioral response. A great deal of research has been conducted on prompting with students with ASD, including studies on effective prompts, the appropriate timing of prompts, and how to fade prompts. One evidence-based prompting strategy that can be effective during instruction is least-to-most prompts (Neitzel & Wolrey, 2008). Teachers arrange prompts from the least to most intrusive, beginning with the lowest level of prompting and proceeding to prompts that offer more assistance if students are not successful. After selecting the target skill (e.g., writing the response to a math problem) teachers need to decide what type of prompt in the prompting hierarchy should be given. Least-to-most prompts may follow this hierarchy:

Gestural
Verbal (full, partial)
Visual
Model (full, partial)
Physical (full, partial; Neitzel & Wolery, 2008)

If students respond correctly after receiving a cue or instruction, they can be reinforced. If students do not respond or respond incorrectly, teachers can provide prompts based on the given hierarchy, ensuring eventual success for the student.

Several other prompting strategies, including simultaneous prompting and time delay, may assist students with ASD in successfully responding. When using simultaneous prompting, instructors provide a *controlling prompt* for the student directly after the cue is given. A controlling prompt is a type of prompt that ensures a correct response from the student. For example, an educator shows a student a picture of a car, then asks the student, "What is this?" and immediately responds "a car." The educator's response with the correct answer is the controlling prompt. A controlling prompt is used during instructional sessions, whereas an independent response is expected from the student during probe sessions (Akmanoglu & Batu, 2004). Time delay is a practice that focuses on fading prompts during instructional activities (Neitzel, 2009). Used in conjunction with the prompting procedures described previously, a brief time delay is provided between the cue and any additional instructions or prompts. For example, a teacher might provide a simultaneous prompt when a student with ASD is initially learning a skill. The educator gradually increases the waiting time between the cue and the prompt as the student becomes more proficient at using the skill (Neitzel, 2009).

Reinforcement

Reinforcement, both positive and negative, is used to increase the use of a target skill or behavior. Positive reinforcement is the contingent presentation of a reinforcer immediately following a student's use of the target skill (Neitzel, 2008). The relationship between the student using the target skill and receiving positive reinforcement increases the student's likelihood of demonstrating the target skill again. Teachers must first establish a target skill and performance criteria to effectively use positive reinforcement. For example: *Kate will respond to the cue "Where is the dog?" with only gestural prompts for 3 consecutive days.* Next teachers need to identify meaningful positive reinforcers for individual students. These may be primary reinforcers such as snacks or secondary reinforcers like social praise or preferred activities. When selecting appropriate reinforcers, use a reinforcer checklist and consider the age and interests of the students as well as the targeted skill. More information about reinforcer checklists can be found in the Internet Resources section at the end of this chapter. Once the target skill, performance criteria, and reinforcers are identified, teachers may begin implementing positive reinforcement during instruction. For example, when the teacher provides the cue, "Kate, where is the dog?" and Kate responds correctly with only gestural prompts for assistance, the teacher immediately provides a meaningful reinforcer (e.g., a token that may later be exchanged for time on the computer). After the stated performance criteria is met, a new criteria that is more challenging, such as "Kate will respond correctly with no prompts," is established. Reinforcement is provided when the new skill is demonstrated.

Negative reinforcement is the removal of a stimulus (i.e., something that is aversive to the learner) after a learner with ASD uses a target skill/behavior or skill. For example, a student may be required to take several bites of lunch before she is permitted to leave the cafeteria. The cafeteria is the "aversive" stimulus in this example and it is removed (e.g., student can leave) when the student has demonstrated the target behavior (taking bites). Other examples include allowing students to leave their desk once math problems are completed (i.e., completing math problems is the target behavior and the desk is the aversive stimulus) and permitting a student to skip a test on Friday if all weekly homework is turned in on time (i.e., turning in weekly homework is the target behavior and the test is the aversive stimulus).

It is essential that data be systematically collected when using reinforcement to ensure that indeed the target behavior or skill is increasing. An educator may select and provide a special activity or item to students after a desired behavior is demonstrated; however, if that behavior does not occur more frequently, the item would not be deemed a reinforcer. For example, data indicate a student rarely greets peers or staff when entering the classroom (two times per day). Educators decide that each time the student greets someone, he will receive a sticker. After 2 weeks of consistent sticker use, when data are collected again on this behavior, staff realizes that the student continues to greet staff and peers approximately only two times per day. The stickers are not a reinforcement for this student. Data collection strategies, as described in the previous chapter, are a key component of systematic instruction to ensure that the strategies selected are effective.

Chaining

Skills may be taught as discrete tasks—one that requires only a single response from students—or as chained tasks, those that require a sequence of steps for completion. The steps in a task analysis form a behavioral chain that can be taught, such as all of the links in the "chain" of steps required to wash hands, prepare a meal, or get dressed. When the sequence of behaviors occurs correctly, students are reinforced. Initially students are reinforced after completing each step of the task. As steps are mastered, students are reinforced only when successfully completing two steps of the sequence, then when three steps are completed correctly, and so on. This strategy, reinforcing responses that occur in a sequence to form more complex behavior, is called chaining. Chaining can be used across curriculum areas and is particularly effective when teaching students with ASD (Hall, 2008).

Shaping

Another component of systematic instruction is shaping, which is both an instructional and a reinforcement strategy. When using shaping, educators reinforce a student's attempts towards or successive approximations of a desired target behavior. For example, when teaching handwriting, teachers may select the target behavior of successfully writing a specific letter. Initially students may be provided with visual cues to assist with tracing the letters. After tracing, students are reinforced, as tracing is an intermediate behavior on the way to the target behavior of writing. These behaviors are reinforced until established, and then new intermediate behaviors are identified and reinforced (e.g., tracing a letter with fewer cues, writing a portion of the letter independently). Finally, the behavior has been shaped and the target behavior of writing a letter independently is expected and reinforced (Alberto & Troutman, 2006).

Using Systematic Instruction (Task Analysis, Prompting, Positive Reinforcement, and Chaining) to Support Students With ASD During Technology Instruction

Ms. Sam, an inclusion support teacher working with students with moderate disabilities, was trying to encourage the students with ASD to access their reading programs on the computer. When the students arrived at the computer during technology class, however, they were often unengaged, off-task, and didn't seem to know where to begin. Ms. Sam realized that perhaps the students didn't know how to find the appropriate programs on the computer desktop and she decided this needed to be a piece of the technology instruction. Working with the general education teacher, she first developed a task analysis related to finding, opening, and beginning the reading computer program:

1. *Press the computer power button.*
2. *Press the monitor power button.*
3. *Place hand on the mouse.*
4. *Move the cursor with the mouse until it points to the Kidspiration® icon.*
5. *Double click the Kidspiration ® icon.*
6. *Move the cursor with the mouse to the Sign In box.*
7. *Left click in the box.*
8. *Type in your name (use visual cue if needed).*

9. *Place hand back on mouse.*
10. *Move cursor to the box labeled "Beginning letters."*
11. *Single click the box.*
12. *Begin activity.*

Then she and the general education teacher began teaching the steps to their students using a least-to-most prompting hierarchy. Ms. Sam started by using gestures to direct her students' attention to the correct location on the computer or screen. If students didn't respond to the gestural prompt she then added a verbal instruction, "Press the power button." If a student still was not able to respond she would either push the button for the student and model the skill or physically help the student to push the button. Initially she reinforced students after completing step one ("Good work, Keisha!"or providing a primary reinforcer). When that was mastered she reinforced the students after completing steps one and two ("Way to go--the computer is on!"). Slowly, as students mastered additional steps of the behavioral chain Ms. Sam was able to reinforce less frequently until the students were able to demonstrate this skill independently. Using task analysis, prompting, reinforcement, and chaining, Ms. Sam was able to effectively instruct her students how to access their literacy practice on the computer (Hume, 2010).

Generalization and Independence

Implementing the instructional strategies described in this chapter will likely increase a student's engagement during instruction. A challenge arises, however, for students with ASD as they leave the setting in which instruction took place and attempt to apply the skills in a new setting, with new materials, or with new people. Students with autism have difficulty generalizing new skills to new contexts (Hall, 2008). Challenges in generalization may be present for several reasons, including poor flexibility, difficulty relating new stimuli to past experiences, and lack of responsiveness to cues (Fein, Tinder, & Waterhouse, 1979). Instructional strategies must include support for these generalization difficulties. Students should have multiple opportunities to practice their skills in a number of environments using a variety of materials and with a number of peers and adults. For example, when presented with a series of 10 flash cards to put in alphabetical order Andrew, a 7-year-old with Asperger's syndrome, put them in order perfectly each time. The teacher thought he had the skill of alphabetizing mastered until she presented Andrew with a new group of 10 words. He did not know where to start. Once the teacher showed him the order of the words he memorized it and could order them correctly on his own, but he did not understand the concept of alphabetical order. Using multiple examples also ensures that students are becoming familiar with materials that they will encounter outside of the classroom in generalization settings. If students are able to alphabetize flash cards as well as names in a phone book, CDs on a CD rack, and authors on a library shelf it is more likely that the skill of alphabetizing will generalize when students are faced with these tasks and materials outside of the instructional setting (Hume, 2010).

Instruction must also include strategies to enhance independent performance. These may include a planned effort to reduce teacher prompting as quickly as possible (e.g., utilizing the "least" prompts whenever possible) or the amount of reinforcement provided and instead embed reinforcement in the curricular materials. Teachers can also implement self-management strategies during instruction. These strategies teach students how to monitor and record their own behavior on a target skill and then reinforce themselves when agreed upon performance criteria are met (Alberto & Troutman, 2006).

Using Systematic Instruction (Self-Management) to Support Students During Literacy Instruction

Ms. Hatton was worried about how her student with autism would do next year when he went from his fifth-grade class at Mountain Shadows to middle school. As long as Ms. Hatton was right on top of Karl he could complete most literacy activities, even editing his essays. If she was helping another student, however, Karl was typically off-task and unengaged while students went through the editing process. She decided to implement some self-management strategies with Karl. She selected a target goal for Karl that included editing his essays for punctuation, capitalization, spacing, and correct headings. She developed a checklist for him that asked questions such as "Have I put a period at the end of sentences?" and "Have I capitalized the first word of each sentence?" She added a spot for him to check off each question as he completed the editing. She then taught him how to use the self-recording tool and they agreed upon reinforcement if the editing was completed independently and accurately. Ms. Hatton was pleasantly surprised how well the self-management strategies worked in supporting Karl's independence during literacy activities and she was much more hopeful about his upcoming transition to middle school.

Summary

Students with ASD have often been left out of instruction due to the use of instructional strategies that are not well-matched to their unique learning needs and characteristics (e.g., creative play, modeling, conversation; Smith, 2001). The field has recognized, however, that students with ASD can benefit tremendously from classroom instruction if presented in a systematic manner. These benefits are more likely to occur if educators are thoughtful about how alterations in instruction may improve the skills of their students with ASD.

References

Akmanoglu, N., & Batu, S. (2004). Teaching pointing to numerals to individuals with autism using simultaneous prompting. *Education and Training in Developmental Disabilities, 39,* 326-336.

Alberto, P., & Troutman, A. (2006). *Applied behavior analysis for teachers.* Upper Saddle River, NJ: Pearson Education.

Boutot, A., & Hume, K. (2010). *Beyond time out and table time: Today's Applied Behavior Analysis for students with autism.* Arlington, VA: Council for Exceptional Children, Division on Autism and Developmental Disabilities. Available online at http://www.daddcec.org/positionpapers

Bulgren, J., & Carta, J. (1993). Examining the instructional contexts of students with learning disabilities. *Exceptional Children, 59,* 182-191.

Fein, D., Tinder, P., & Waterhouse, L. (1979), Stimulus generalization in autistic and normal children. *Journal of Child Psychology and Psychiatry, 20,* 325–335.

Hall, L. (2008). *Autism Spectrum Disorders: From theory to practice.* Upper Saddle River, NJ: Pearson.

Hill, E. (2004). Executive dysfunction in autism. *TRENDS in Cognitive Sciences, 8,* 26-32.

Hume, K. (2010). Effective instructional strategies for students with ASD: Keys to enhancing literacy instruction. In C. Carnahan & P. Williamson (Eds.), *Quality literacy instruction for students with autism spectrum disorders.* Shawnee Mission, KS: AAPC.

Iovannone, R., Dunlap, G., Huber, H., & Kincaid, D. (2003). Effective educational practices for students with autism spectrum disorders. *Focus on Autism and Other Developmental Disabilities, 18,* 150-166.

Neitzel, J. (2008). *Positive reinforcement: Steps for implementation.* Chapel Hill, NC: National Professional Development Center on Autism Spectrum Disorders, Frank Porter Graham Child Development Institute, The University of North Carolina at Chapel Hill.

Neitzel, J. (2009). *Overview of time delay.* Chapel Hill, NC: National Professional Development Center on Autism Spectrum Disorders, Frank Porter Graham Child Development Institute, The University of North Carolina.

Neitzel, J., & Wolery, M. (2008). *Least-to-most prompting: Steps for implementation.* Chapel Hill, NC: National Professional Development Center on Autism Spectrum Disorders, Frank Porter Graham Child Development Institute, The University of North Carolina at Chapel Hill.

Odom, S., Collet-Klinenberg, L., Rogers, S., & Hatton, D. (2010). Evidence-based practices in interventions for children and youth with autism spectrum disorders. *Preventing School Failure, 54,* 275-282.

Smith, T. (2001). Discrete trial training in the treatment of autism. *Focus on Autism and Other Developmental Disorders, 16,* 86-92.

Internet Resources

http://autismpdc .fpg.unc.edu/
Web site for National Professional Development Center on ASD which provides detailed descriptions of practices, steps for implementation, and data collection tools.

http://www.autisminternetmodules.org
Autism Internet Modules, 23 interactive online modules which describe a number of evidence-based practices and offers video/photo examples.

http://www.behavioradvisor.com/TaskAnalysis.html
Provides additional examples of task analysis sequences.

http://www.lessons4all.org/downloads /reinforcement_checklist.pdf
Provides a thorough reinforcer checklist.

Functional Communication Training

Robert C. Pennington and G. Rich Mancil

One of the diagnostic criteria for autism is impairment in communicative functioning. Researchers have reported that many children with autism spectrum disorders (ASD) do not acquire a functional communication system (Miranda-Linne & Melin, 1997). As a result, children with ASD may learn to engage in challenging behavior in lieu of using conventional communication (Bott, Farmer, & Rhode 1997; Chung, Jenner, Chamberlain, & Corbett. 1995, Sigafoos, 2000). If unaddressed, these problem behaviors may serve as barriers to success across a wide range of contexts (e.g., school, community, vocational). In addition, these problem behaviors are likely to increase in severity as children grow older.

Researchers and practitioners have applied a variety of interventions to address challenging behavior exhibited by people with autism (Machalicek, O'Reilly, Beretvas, Sigafoos, & Lancioni, 2007). Unfortunately, many of the interventions implemented in the studies reviewed by Machalicek et al. (2007) failed to address the lack of communication skills that may be at the core of the challenging behavior. Consequently, students may continue to use challenging behavior to express their wants and needs. One promising intervention that simultaneously addresses communication needs and challenging behavior is functional communication training (FCT). Functional communication training is a procedure in which students learn communication skills to replace their challenging behaviors. Researchers have demonstrated that students maintain new skills acquired through FCT and may apply them in new contexts (Durand & Carr, 1992).

Implementing Functional Communication Training

Functional communication training consists of three major components. First, a team of educational professionals conducts a functional behavior assessment to determine the function of the problem behavior. Second, the team selects an effective communicative response that serves the same function as the problem behavior. This response must be easy for the student to perform and able to be clearly understood by those around him/ her. In other words, using appropriate communication must become an easier route to desired reinforcers than engaging in problem behavior. Finally, the team develops and implements a behavior support plan. During implementation it is critical that team members monitor progress and make revisions to the plan as needed.

Conducting a Functional Behavior Assessment

In the simplest terms, a functional behavior assessment (FBA) addresses the question, "How does the student benefit by engaging in this behavior?" The answer should fall into one of two categories of reinforcers. The student may access preferred stimuli (e.g., attention, tangible item, sensory experience) or they may escape some aversive experience (e.g., difficult task, loud gymnasium, nonpreferred activity). The identification of these reinforcers is critical to the success of any intervention plan involving FCT and therefore, FBA must be thoughtfully planned and conducted. Typically, FBA consists of three major components including indirect assessment, direct observation, and the development of a hypothesis statement.

Indirect Assessments. Indirect assessments use interviews, rating scales/check-lists, and questionnaires to collect information from persons familiar with the student exhibiting the problem behavior. The data collected should provide a description of the challenging behavior and the context in which it occurs. Interview formats range from informal discussions with staff or students to published lists of interview questions (e.g., Functional Assessment Interview [FAI]; O'Neill et al., 1997). One advantage to conducting an interview is that the interviewer can probe for more detail (Mancil & Boman, 2010). Professionals may also use questionnaires or rating scales to gather information about the problem behavior. In general, indirect assessment can provide valuable information, particularly in refining the definition of the challenging behavior and pinpointing times of day and activities in which to conduct direct assessments such as antecedent-behavior-consequence (ABC) recording. However, indirect assessment alone is not sufficient to determine the cause of a problem behavior. Teachers must consider that those reporting about a student's behavior are doing so through the filter of their own bias.

Direct Observation. The teacher or other staff member then conducts direct observation of the student in those contexts in which the problem behavior occurs. During direct observation, the observer records the frequency, duration, and/or intensity of the problem; teachers can use narrative or continuous ABC data collection. When using narrative recording, the teacher constructs a narrative describing what happened each time the behavior occurs, and includes all relevant antecedent and consequent events. When using continuous recording, the teacher records what happens when the behavior does and does not occur. The continuous ABC data sheet is divided into equal intervals of time and the observer marks antecedent and consequent events using a coded system. Table 5-1 depicts the same instance of a problem behavior using first narrative and then continuous ABC data collection.

Despite the recording method selected, it is critical that the teacher conduct a minimum of three observations to establish the student's pattern of behavior. Following the observation, the team analyzes the data to look for relationships between events in the environment and the occurrence of the behavior. Based on data from these observations and indirect assessment tools, the team members make a guess as to what variables may be responsible for maintaining the problem behavior. For example, after reviewing the data presented in Table 5-1, the teacher might notice that each time the problem behavior occurs, it is preceded by a request to start a difficult task and is followed by a form of escape from the task. The teacher might posit that a relationship exists between avoiding task demands and the problem behavior.

Hypothesis Statement. The next step of the FBA process is to develop a hypothesis statement. The hypothesis statement requires the teacher and other team members to focus on the important variables that will be manipulated during intervention (Cooper, Heron, & Heward, 2007). For the previous example, the teacher might construct the statement, "When Julie is presented with difficult tasks, she scratches the teacher to avoid the task." This calls attention to those conditions that might occasion Julie's problem behavior and those consequences that might maintain them. Once the hypothesis statement is formulated, the teacher tests the hypothesis by implementing an intervention that addresses that function.

Selecting a Communicative Response

Once the FBA has been conducted, the teacher selects a communicative response that matches the hypothesized function of the challenging behavior (Gibson, Pennington, Stenhoff, & Hopper, 2010). For instance, if the hypothesized function of a student's behavior is to escape difficult tasks, the teacher might consider training a communicative response that results in a short break from task demands (e.g., asking for a break). Four general criteria should be considered when selecting a new communicative response to teach to a student (Mancil & Boman, 2010). First, the response should require minimal effort to perform, and substantially less effort to perform than the problem behavior (Horner & Day, 1991). Again, functional communication training renders the challenging behavior as less efficient and effective as the novel response in accessing reinforcement. Second, the teacher should consider the complexity of the response and how easy it will be to teach. It is important that the student acquire the new responses rapidly. For example, a student initially should make a single response (e.g., one word, a single sign, exchange of a single picture) to communicate an entire message. Third, it is critical to select a response that other individuals in the student's immediate environment can understand. For instance, if selecting a signed response, it is important that individuals that most frequently interact with the student understand sign language so that they may reinforce those responses consistently. Finally, the teacher should look beyond the classroom context and consider how effective the response is within the community at large. The teacher should select communicative responses that are easy to perform with minimal support, understood by the lay community, and require augmentative and alternative communication (AAC) tools that are portable.

Table 5-1

ABC Recording

Narrative ABC Recording

Date/Time: 4/22 8:03   **Setting:** Math Room   **Observer:** J.T.

Antecedent	Behavior	Consequence
Mrs. Courtade sits next to Julie, presents a worksheet, and says "Time to work"	*Julie scratches the teacher's hands*	*Mrs. Courtade jumps ups and leaves Julie at the table to work alone*

Continuous ABC Recording

Date/Time: 4/22 8:03   **Setting:** Math Room   **Observer:** J.T.

Time: 8:00-8:05	Antecedent	Behavior	Consequence
	■ Task Demand	■ Physical Aggression	■ Escape
	☐ Tangible removed	☐ Vocal Outburst	☐ Attention
	☐ Working Alone		☐ No response

Developing and Implementing a Treatment Plan

Once the communicative response has been selected, an intervention plan is designed to teach the student to use it across contexts. Initially, the new response is taught using discrete trial training procedures. These procedures typically involve the presentation of multiple opportunities for the student to perform the desired response and access reinforcement in a controlled setting. During the discrete trial training opportunities, the teacher prompts the student to use the new communicative response until the student meets a predetermined criterion for mastery. Once the student has acquired the new response, reinforcement is withheld following problem behavior.

Finally, the teacher assesses the student's generalization of the new communicative response in other contexts. These contexts may include other classrooms or activities, different instructors, and the presence of different preferred or aversive stimuli. Explicit instruction for generalization should be conducted if communicative responses are not observed in untrained contexts (Stokes & Baer, 1977).

A Case Example

Becky, an 8-year-old student with autism, screams frequently during academic tasks. The classroom teacher calls Mrs. Kirkham, a special education teacher, to assess the situation and come up with a solution. Mrs. Kirkham suggests that they conduct an FBA and asks the teacher if she can meet with her after school. During the meeting, the teachers discuss Becky's areas of strengths and needs. It becomes apparent to Mrs. Kirkham that although Becky is using an AAC device to communicate, she has a limited repertoire of responses. Next, Mrs. Kirkham and the teacher agree that Mrs. Kirkham should conduct a formal interview to ascertain when and where the behavior occurs and what events most often precede and follow the problem behavior. The classroom teacher reports that the screaming consistently occurs daily during two periods of seated work tasks. Mrs. Kirkham and the teacher decide that Mrs. Kirkham should schedule three observations during these seated work periods.

Across the next few days, Mrs. Kirkham collects ABC data during three 30-minute observations. She focuses on two dimensions of the problem situation. First, how often Becky's problem behavior occurs, and second, what happens before and after the behavior occurs. After each observation, she plots the frequency of the screaming behavior on a line graph. After the final observation, she reviews data from the interview (i.e., indirect assessment) and her direct observations. She notes that Becky only screams during some tasks. After a follow-up discussion with the classroom teacher, they both agree that Becky screams most often during novel or more difficult tasks. Mrs. Kirkham also notices that Becky's screaming is consistently followed by teacher attention in the form of assistance. Mrs. Kirkham hypothesizes that Becky screams to get assistance during difficult tasks.

After reviewing the baseline data, Mrs. Kirkham and the classroom teacher decide to proceed with intervention. Mrs. Kirkham calls a team meeting to discuss intervention strategies. The team, consisting of the classroom teacher, speech language pathologist, the classroom paraprofessional, and Becky's mother, comes to consensus that Becky's limited communication repertoire may contribute to her vocal outbursts. They decide to use FCT, to teach Becky to request help during academic tasks. Since, Becky has already acquired some responses using her VOCA (Voice Output Communication Aid), the team decides to program a "help" response into her device.

Mrs. Kirkham decides to teach the new response using a discrete trial method. Instructional sessions begin in a 1:1 arrangement within the special education resource room. She starts by engineering opportunities for Becky to request assistance. Mrs. Kirkham develops worksheets comprised of simple (mastered) items and a few embedded items designed to be impossible to complete without assistance. She uses constant time delay to teach Becky to request help. During the first instructional session, Mrs. Kirkham prompts Becky to press the help button on her VOCA immediately after reading the challenging item. She then delivers assistance and praises Becky for completing the item. During the next session, Mrs. Kirkham inserts a 5-second delay between reading the item and prompting the "help" response. After Becky independently requests help (i.e., before the prompt) on 100% of the contrived opportunities, the team introduces the contrived opportunities within the general education classroom seatwork activities.

Prior to this next step, Mrs. Kirkham instructs the classroom teacher and teacher assistant on how to implement FCT procedures. After introduction of the intervention in the classroom setting, Mrs. Kirkham observes the staff implementing the training procedures and provides feedback to ensure FCT is implemented as planned. Once Becky selects the "help" button on her VOCA consistently in the general education classroom, Mrs. Kirkham directs the staff to withhold assistance following problem behavior. Instead, they are directed to wait until the screaming subsides, prompt the "help" response, and then provide assistance.

The staff continues to collect frequency data on Becky's screaming behavior and her use of the "help response." After a week of intervention, the staff observes a sharp decrease in the screaming behavior and a corresponding increase in "help" response. The staff slowly fades the contrived trials and continues to monitor the behavior as Becky is exposed to new contexts.

Keys to Success

When implementing FCT, it is critical that the teacher consider several factors to ensure success. First, the teacher must enlist key players in implementing the FCT program. It is important that all staff respond to the new response and the problem behavior in the same way. During FCT, the student must learn that the new response is effective across personnel and that the problem behavior will no longer result in reinforcement from anyone. In addition, the success in FCT across communicative partners may increase the likelihood that the student will communicate with new personnel.

Second, any behavior change program should be accompanied by the collection of continuous data. When collecting ongoing data, the teacher should plot data on a line graph each day. Line graphs provide teachers the opportunity to notice subtle changes in student performance that may be difficult to extrapolate from raw data. Line graphs also can be used to clearly communicate student progress to other team members. Teachers must establish baseline levels of problem behavior prior to starting intervention. Baseline levels of performance are determined by analyzing data collected across a minimum of three different observations. Data can be obtained during the FBA process to reduce any delay in starting intervention. It is important that teachers, eager to start intervention, do not overlook this critical step. During intervention, behavior change may be gradual and not easily observed without a baseline condition in which to compare it.

In addition, it is important that during intervention, the teacher collects data on the occurrence of the new communicative response and the problem behavior. These data provide useful information concerning the effectiveness of the new response in replacing the problem behavior. The data should indicate that as the frequency of the new response increases, the problem behavior decreases. If this is not the case, the teacher needs to consider whether the student requires more training on using the new response or whether the new response actually serves the same function as the problem behavior.

Summary

Researchers have demonstrated that FCT is an evidence-based practice for students with ASD. This powerful intervention has many benefits over traditional behavior reductive techniques (e.g., time-out, response cost). The use of FCT may expand students' communicative repertoires thus increasing their autonomy within their environment and ultimately improving their quality of life.

References

Bott, C., Farmer, R., & Rhode, J. (1997). Behavior problems associated with lack of speech in people with learning disabilities. *Journal of Intellectual Disability Research, 41,* 3-17.

Chung, M. C., Jenner, L., Chamberlain, L., & Corbett, J. (1995). One-year follow-up pilot study on communication skill and challenging behavior. *European Journal of Psychiatry, 9,* 83–95.

Cooper, J. O., Heron, T. E., & Heward, W. L. (2007). *Applied behavior analysis.* Upper Saddle River, NJ: Pearson.

Durand, V. M., & Carr, E. G. (1992). An analysis of maintenance following functional communication training. *Journal of Applied Behavior Analysis, 25,* 777-794.

Gibson, J. L., Pennington, R. C., Stenhoff, D. M., & Hopper, J. S. (2010). Using videoconferencing to deliver interventions to a preschool student with autism. *Topics in Early Childhood Special Education, 29,* 214-225.

Horner, R. H., & Day, H. M. (1991). The effects of response efficiency on functionally equivalent competing behaviors. *Journal of Applied Behavior Analysis, 24,* 719-732.

Kokina, A., & Kern, L. (2010). Social story interventions for students with autism spectrum disorders: A meta analysis. *Journal of Autism and Developmental Disorders, 40,* 812-826.

Lee, S., Simpson, R. L., & Shogren, K. A. (2007). Effects and implications of self-management for students with autism: A meta-analysis. *Focus on Autism and Other Developmental Disabilities, 22,* 2-13.

Love, J. R., Carr, J. E., & LeBlanc, L. A. (2008). Functional assessment of problem behavior in children with autism spectrum disorders: A summary of 32 outpatient cases. *Journal of Autism and Developmental Disorders, 39,* 363, 372.

Machalicek, W., O'Reilly, M. F., Beretvas, N., Sigafoos, J., & Lancioni, G. E. (2007). A review of interventions to reduce challenging behavior in school settings for students with autism spectrum disorders. *Research in Autism Spectrum Disorders, 1,* 229-246.

Mancil, G. R. (2006). Functional communication training: A review of the literature related to autism. *Education and Training in Developmental Disabilities, 41,* 213-224.

Mancil, G. R., & Boman, M. (2010). Functional Communication training in the classroom: A guide for success. *Preventing School Failure, 54,* 238-246.

Miranda-Linne, F. M., & Melin, L. (1997). A comparison of speaking and mute individuals with autism and autism-like conditions on the autism behavior checklist. *Journal of Autism and Developmental Disorders, 27,* 245-264.

O'Neill, R. E., Horner, R. H., Albin, R. W., Sprague, J. R., Storey, K., & Newton, J. S. (1997). *Functional assessment and program development for problem behavior: A practical handbook.* Pacific Grove, CA: Brooks/Cole.

Sigafoos, J. (2000). Communication development and aberrant behavior in children with developmental disabilities. *Education and Training in Mental Retardation and Developmental Disabilities, 35,* 168–176.

Stokes, T. F., & Baer, D. M. (1977). An implicit technology of generalization. *Journal of Applied Behavior Analysis, 10,* 349-367.

Additional Resources by Topic

Functional Communication Training

Mancil, G. R., & Boman, M. (2010). Functional Communication training in the classroom: A guide for success. *Preventing School Failure, 54,* 238-246.

Reichle, J., & Wacker, D. (Eds.). (1993). *Communicative alternatives to challenging behavior: Integrating functional assessment and intervention strategies.* Baltimore, MD: Brookes.

Functional Behavioral Assessment

Functional Assessment Screening Tool

Iwata, B. A. (1995). *Functional assessment screening tool.* Gainesville, FL: The Florida Center on Self-Injury.

Questions About Behavioral Function

Matson J. L., & Vollmer T. R. (1995). *User's guide: Questions about behavioral function (QABF).* Baton Rouge, LA: Scientific.

Motivational Assessment Scale

Durand, V. M., & Crimmins, D. B. (1998). Identifying the variables maintaining self-injurious behavior. *Journal of Autism and Developmental Disorders, 18,* 99-117.

Carr, J. E., & Wilder, D. A. (2003). *Functional assessment and intervention.* Homewood, IL: High Tide Disability Press.

O'Neill, R., Horner, R., Albin, R., Storey, K., & Sprague, J. (1990). *Functional assessment and program development for problem behavior: A practical handbook.* Stamford, CT: Wadsworth.

Constant Time Delay

Stevens, K. B., & Lingo, A. S. (2005). Constant time delay: One way to provide positive behavioral supports for students with emotional and behavioral disabilities. *Beyond Behavior, 15,* 10-15.

Naturalistic Interventions

G. Rich Mancil

When first hearing the term *naturalistic interventions*, one may wonder what this entails. Does it refer to interventions done in natural settings such as homes and classrooms, or to how interventions are implemented in these aforementioned contexts? The answer is a little of both. Naturalistic interventions are a collection of practices like environmental arrangements, interaction techniques, and behavioral strategies that are implemented in natural settings. Some researchers and practitioners in the field of autism spectrum disorders (ASD) use the term incidental teaching interchangeably with natural interventions (Mancil, 2009), while others purport it is merely one of the practices within naturalistic interventions along with milieu therapy and embedded instruction (Mancil, 2009).

The overall approach of naturalistic interventions is to address target skills of learners by using their interests to guide interventions and instruction. The idea is to build more complex skills by using these interests that are naturally reinforcing and fit within the typical interactions in settings. Baer consistently mentioned that for behavior change to be effective and maintained, the new behaviors must come into contact with naturally occurring reinforcers (Stokes & Baer, 1977).

Basic Steps in Implementing Naturalistic Interventions

When implementing naturalistic interventions (Cowan & Allen, 2007), the basic steps include (a) identifying the skill to be taught, (b) choosing the appropriate context (classroom, playground, etc.), (c) choosing particular strategies/procedures to use, (d) training all pertinent staff, (e) implementing the intervention, and (f) tracking data and making changes as needed. These steps are shown in Figure 6-1 and will be described in detail in a case study.

Figure 6-1

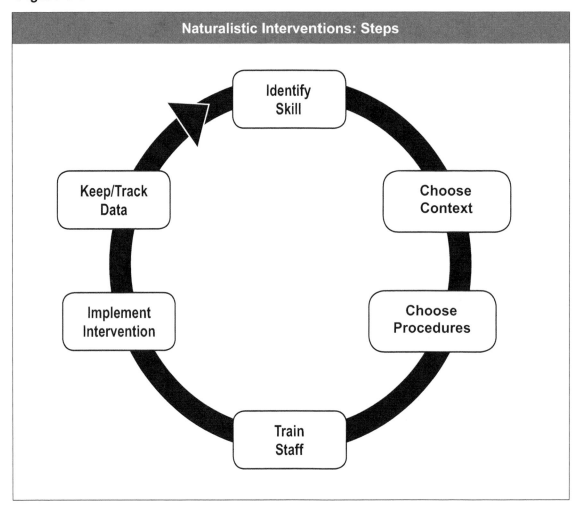

Naturalistic Interventions: Steps

Identify Skill

Choose Context

Choose Procedures

Train Staff

Implement Intervention

Keep/Track Data

Naturalistic Intervention Strategies

The four procedures typically used to teach the skills through naturalistic interventions are: (a) modeling, (b) mand-modeling, (c) time delay, and (d) incidental teaching. Each procedure is discussed in the following sections.

Modeling

One of the naturalistic intervention strategies used to promote communication and other skill development in natural environments is modeling correct responses and correcting the target student's responses. This involves modeling a target behavior and then providing corrections to the student as necessary (Alpert & Kaiser, 1992). For example, while outside on the playground, a child may tap on the adult's arm and look at the toy dump truck. The adult gains the child's attention and provides a verbal prompt that matches the child's communication skill level, such as *Want truck?* If the child says, *Want truck,* the adult provides praise, repeats the child's phrase (e.g., says, *Yes, want truck*) and gives the child the toy dump truck. Otherwise, the adult provides a corrective model repeatedly, *Want truck* until the target child correctly models the response. However, if the child does not respond in a reasonable time frame (e.g., 2 to 3 seconds), as predetermined by the researcher, parent, and/or teacher, the adult provides a model and gives the object to the child. The purpose of modeling and correcting responses is to provide the target child the necessary prompts and instructions in natural situations to assist in skill development.

Mand-Modeling

Another component typically utilized in naturalistic interventions is the mand-model technique. The mand-model technique involves giving a direct instruction within a naturally occurring activity and context (Charlop & Walsh, 1986). The mand is a vocal operant that is maintained by a reinforcer (e.g., obtaining a preferred item such as a toy car) and is evoked by the discriminative stimuli for that reinforcer (Skinner, 1957). For example, if a student says, *Water please* and receives the water, it is likely that this is a mand. Also, it is important to recognize that responses are deemed mands based on their controlling variables and not on their topography. Sign language and picture cards can function as mands the same as vocal responses function as mands. When necessary, this mand would be followed by a model and a correction similar to the previous description. The mand-model is performed by first gaining the student's attention and then providing a prompt for a target behavior. After the prompt, a guided model (i.e., assisting the student in performing the target behavior) is provided when necessary. For instance, a child is given apple juice for snack and reaches to pick it up with his hands. The adult provides a response block (e.g., blocks his hands), obtains the child's attention, and says, *Tell me what you want* (prompting a mand), places the communication card with the picture of juice on it in the child's hand, and physically guides his hand to the adult who has the apple juice (corrective model). If the child continues to ask for juice by using the picture card, the adult provides the juice paired with positive praise (e.g., *Good job asking*). If the child attempts to grab the juice again without using the communication card, the adult repeats the process. The purpose of the mand-model strategy is to develop independent skills by providing the student with a prompt for the mand and an example of performing the communicative response correctly. The adult continues with this procedure until a performance criterion is met (e.g., student performs the task correctly for 2 days).

Time Delay

Time delay is another procedure often used in naturalistic contexts that involves the adult providing a stimulus and then waiting approximately 5 to 30 seconds, for a student-initiated response (Kaiser, 1993). Time delay typically is combined with other techniques such as the mand-model. If the student does not respond, the adult provides a mand-model. For example, a student may want his coat, but needs help getting it from the shelf. While attending to the student, the adult waits for a period of 5 to 30 seconds for him to request help. If the student requests by using a communicative response such as a picture card or vocalization, the adult provides him with the requested item. If the student does not independently request help within the time delay, the adult provides a mand-model. The amount of time delay chosen depends on the student's level. The longer the wait period, the greater the chance of losing the student's interest; therefore, care is needed in choosing the appropriate time delay. The purpose of time delay is to decrease the student's dependence on adult prompting, instructions, and models; thus, promoting independent and spontaneous (i.e., unprompted) communication.

Incidental Teaching

Incidental teaching is another strategy often employed within the framework of naturalistic interventions. Incidental teaching is a process in which communication skills are learned in naturally occurring interactions or when interactions are arranged in natural contexts. This may be the reason the terms, incidental teaching and milieu therapy, have been used interchangeably at times. Hart and Risley (1968; 1975) described incidental teaching as an interaction between an adult (e.g., parent) and a child during unstructured situations such as free play where the child controls the incidences in which teaching occurs by signaling interest in the environment. For example, while playing with toy cars, a child may point to a car and say, *ca*. The adult reinforces this behavior by giving the child the toy car. Incidental teaching typically is combined with the other procedures and is applied during situations when children are requesting either vocally or nonvocally. Prompts are provided if necessary. Further, access to desired objects is contingent upon correct responses, which are followed by behavior specific praise. For example, an adult may create a situation by "accidentally" forgetting to give a child her milk during snack (i.e., sabotaging the environment). The adult then would use the aforementioned techniques to enhance communication by giving a prompt when needed, praising the child for correct responses, and giving the child the milk (contingent access) for correct responses. The purpose of incidental teaching is to promote fluency and expand skills of children with language delays, which may include children with ASD (e.g., Hart & Risley, 1975; Ingersoll, Lewis, & Kroman, 2007; Ingersoll & Schreibman, 2006; MacDuff, Krantz, MacDuff, & McClannahan, 1988).

Case Examples

Case 1: Vladimir

Vladimir is a 4-year old boy with ASD who enjoys playing with Bob the Builder™ toys and building items that he can use with these toys. He is able to speak, but it is difficult to understand what he is saying at times. Vladimir often plays by himself, seldom engaging peers. His teacher and mother both noted, however, that he appears to like other children but does not seem to know how to get them to play with him. His mother also indicated that he plays with his little sister, who is 2-years old, at home. In the preschool classroom, there is a carpeted area that is used for choice activities where children often play with toy cars and blocks.

Given this detailed description, implement the steps and apply the procedures discussed. First, identify the skill to be taught. In this particular case example, two areas may need to be addressed: to improve the understanding of Vladimir's speech and to increase his engagement with peers. For purposes of the example, the focus will be on engaging peers in play.

Second, choose the appropriate context. The context to teach the skill in the natural environment in this case would be the carpeted area in the classroom where children play with toy cars and blocks. Why is this the case? The answer is twofold. First, Vladimir likes to play with Bob the Builder™ toys, which include toy construction equipment with wheels. Second, other children in the classroom play with wheeled toys and blocks in this designated carpet area of the classroom; thus, no setting would have to be contrived to support engagement with peers.

Third, choose particular strategies/procedures to use. In this case, it is best to use incidental teaching with prompting techniques. This may look like the following:

Vladimir's peers may be on the rug playing with Bob the Builder™ toys and other wheeled toys. The teacher could prompt Vladimir to ask a peer if he may play with the Bob the Builder™ toys with him.

Fourth, identify and train all pertinent staff. Because this is being conducted in the classroom, it is important that the teacher train the assistants. The teacher may need to model the procedures several times and role-play with the assistants. After role-playing, the assistants could then implement the procedures with identified students as the teacher probes for accuracy. Keep in mind that additional training sessions may need to occur periodically. Fifth, implement the intervention in a similar manner as described for part three above.

Finally, track data and make changes as needed. Data should be kept on student progress and implementation of the procedures (i.e., treatment fidelity.)

The prior example demonstrates a naturalistic intervention that was applied to help Vladimir engage peers to play with him. Following is another example that depicts a case and describes the implementation of the process. For this example, use the form in the Figure 6-2 to describe each area. For example, what were the skills targeted and what strategies were used?

Figure 6-2

Naturalistic Procedure Form

1. Identify the skill to be taught.

   a.

   b.

2. Choose the appropriate context.

   a.

   b.

3. Choose particular strategies/procedures to use.

   a.

   b.

4. Identify and train pertinent staff.

   a.

   b.

5. Implement the intervention.

   a.

   b.

6. Track data and make changes as needed.

   a.

   b.

Case 2: Landon

Landon is a 5-year-old boy who loves to play with the racecars on the rug. Although he has limited verbal communication, he can point to what he wants, but does not have any systematic form of communication. Landon happens to love a specific racetrack rug. In fact, many children love this type of rug. The rug is typically 3X5 or 4X6 and the design is usually a racetrack or a town with pictures of buildings and a road that goes near each two dimensional structure.

Landon's favorite activity is to follow the road patterns on the rug. He is starting to verbalize a little, such as saying the word car or track. However, these are isolated events not connected to activities. His mother notes that Landon often screams and engages in tantrums for what he wants. Landon's father and the clinician decide to enhance Landon's communication by playing with him on the rug with his racecars. The first step is to have Landon say "car." The first day, they sit at the rug and both Landon and his father have a toy car and they play with them on the track. While they play, the father comments about the car, points to his and Landon's car and says, "Car, I like your car." In addition, the father pretends that his car is not working. He also points to the rug and says, "Racetrack" to encourage Landon to repeat the words after him. After a couple of weeks, Landon consistently repeats his father's words. Landon's father also expands vocabulary by saying, "Blue car" or "Race the car on the track." At first, Landon continues to respond with one word, so the clinician and the father decide to slightly change the activity. While playing with the rug, the father takes Landon's car and prompts Landon to ask for the car. Also, the father lies across the rug and prompts Landon to request the racetrack. Because the track is Landon's special interest, and not the car, this design was effective. However, the intervention is not without some setbacks. The first few times the father sits across the rug, Landon begins crying and throws his car down. But with a few prompts, he begins to successfully request his father to play with him. Over the course of a week Landon consistently requests the car and racetrack without prompts. Landon begins saying, "Play with me, dad." The father encourages further communication by commenting on the colors of the cars and racetrack. After a few months, Landon requests specific cars such as the red car and comments on different features of the racetrack such as pointing to the firehouse and saying, "I like the firehouse" and "That's where firemen work." At the end of the study, the father sits down with the clinician and notes that Landon also began commenting on other items in the house and their characteristics.

Summary

The strategies outlined in this chapter are effective in teaching children communication skills, decreasing dependence on adult prompts, and promoting fluency in language. The interventions are grounded in applied behavior analysis and implemented in natural environments.

References

Alpert, C. L., & Kaiser, A. P. (1992). Training parents as milieu language teachers. *Journal of Early Intervention, 16*, 31-52.

Charlop, M. H., & Walsh, M. E. (1986). Increasing autistic children's spontaneous verbalizations of affection: An assessment of time delay and peer modeling procedures. *Journal of Applied Behavior Analysis, 19*, 307-314.

Cowan, R., & Allen, K. (2007). Using naturalistic procedures to enhance learning in individuals with autism: A focus on generalized teaching within the school setting. *Psychology in the Schools, 44*, 701-715.

Hart, B., & Risley, T. R. (1975). Incidental teaching of language in the preschool. *Journal of Applied Behavior Analysis, 8*, 411-420.

Hart, B. M., & Risley, T. R. (1968). Establishing use of descriptive adjectives in the spontaneous speech of disadvantaged preschool children. *Journal of Applied Behavior Analysis, 1*, 109-120.

Ingersoll, B., Lewis, E., & Kroman, E. (2007). Teaching the imitation and spontaneous use of descriptive gestures in young children with autism using a naturalistic behavioral intervention. *Journal of Autism and Developmental Disorders, 37*, 1446-1456.

Ingersoll, B., & Schreibman, L. (2006). Teaching reciprocal imitation skills to young children with autism using naturalistic behavioral approach: Effects on language, pretend play, and joint attention. *Journal of Autism and Developmental Disorders, 36*, 487-505.

Kaiser, A. P. (1993). Functional language. In M. E. Snell (Ed.), *Instruction of students with severe disabilities* (4th ed., 347-379). New York, NY: Macmillan.

MacDuff, G. S., Krantz, P. J., MacDuff, M. A., & McClannahan, L. E. (1988). Providing incidental teaching for autistic children: A rapid training procedure for therapists. *Education and Treatment of Children, 11*, 205-217.

Mancil, G. R. (2009). Milieu therapy as a communication intervention: A review of the literature related to children with autism spectrum disorder. *Education and Training in Developmental Disabilities, 44,* 105-117.

Skinner, B. F. (1957). *Verbal Behavior.* New York, NY: Appleton-Century-Crofts.

Stokes, T., & Baer, D. (1977). An implicit technology of generalization. *Journal of Applied Behavior Analysis, 10,* 349-367.

Additional Resources

Chawarska, K., Klin, A., Volkmar, F., & Powers, M. (2008). *Autism Spectrum Disorders in infants and toddlers: Diagnosis, assessment, and treatment.* New York, NY: Guilford Press.

Koegel, R., & Koegel, L. (1995). *Teaching children with autism: Strategies for initiating positive interactions and improving learning opportunities.* Baltimore, MD: Paul H. Brookes.

Internet Resource

http://autismpdc.fpg.unc.edu/content/naturalistic-intervention
The National Professional Development Center on Autism Spectrum Disorders provides detailed descriptions of and evidence-based research on naturalistic interventions. The web site also includes steps for implementation, a checklist, and data collections forms.

Increasing Social Skills

Monica E. Delano, Kelly Whalon, and Barbara Y. Wert

Developing social communication skills is inherently challenging for people with an autism spectrum disorders (ASD). Even with early intervention, some social communication difficulties are expected to persist during the school years and beyond (Loveland, & Tunali-Kotoski, 2005). The social communication challenges experienced by children across the autism spectrum will present differently (Loveland & Tunali-Kotoski, 2005), and as a result, social skill instruction should target individual needs (Olley, 2005). Despite this variability, there is some predictability (Loveland & Tunali-Kotoski, 2005) that suggests initiating, responding to, and maintaining interactions with others are generally important instructional targets for learners with ASD (Olley, 2005).

Effective social skill instruction includes opportunities for students with ASD to engage in authentic social interactions in multiple, typical settings throughout the school day (Bellini, Peters, Benner, & Hopf, 2007). Such opportunities provide students with ASD a chance to practice newly acquired skills in natural settings, thereby increasing generalization and maximizing gains (Bellini et al., 2007). If students with ASD are provided little time to socially interact with their general education peers, then time to enhance their social skills is limited (Marans, Rubin, & Laurent, 2005). Yet, even in inclusive settings, minimal time is provided for students with ASD to interact with their peers without disabilities, and access to evidence-based social skill instruction is lacking (Theimann & Kamps, 2008). The effects of insufficient time and opportunity for interaction are compounded by the fact that many social skill interventions are minimally effective (Bellini et al., 2007). Two interventions with research support are *peer-mediated instruction* and *video modeling*.

Peer-Mediated Instruction

Peer-mediated instruction (PMI) is an evidence-based practice that teachers use to increase the social communication of students with ASD (Chan et al., 2009; Wang, Cui, & Parrila, 2011). When implementing this practice, peers without disabilities are taught how to begin and sustain communication with students with ASD (Odom, Collet-Klingenberg, Rogers, & Hatton, 2010). PMI increases the opportunities students with ASD have to interact with their peers, and encourages natural interactions with peers without disabilities without requiring a lot of direct prompting from the teacher (Sperry, Neitzel, & Engelhardt-Wells, 2010). Described as emerging and effective (i.e., evidence from at least six quality single-subject studies; Odom, Collet-Klingenberg et al., 2010), PMI is well supported in the literature, and "should be considered a recommended practice for all individuals with autism" (Reichow & Volkmar, 2010, p. 160).

Eric is 8-years old and in the third grade. He speaks well with good articulation, but he rarely talks, and almost never uses his speech to socially interact with his peers. When Eric speaks, his utterances are short, and typically directed toward an adult to make a request, end a task, or ask for a change in activity. Eric's teacher, Mr. Merit, has noticed that Eric's lack of communication with his peers is isolating him from his classmates. Mr. Merit notices that Eric watches and shows interest in his peers, but does not outwardly initiate an interaction or attempt to join in an activity. Also, Eric does not like loud noises and covers his ears and screams during fire alarms, in the gymnasium and lunchroom. This school year, Eric has yet to eat lunch in the lunchroom with his peers. Recently, Mr. Merit overheard a student describe Eric as "weird." Mr. Merit is concerned that if he does not intervene, Eric will not develop the social communication skills he needs to successfully interact with others, or may even become a target for bullies. In addition, Eric's peers will lose the opportunity to get to know and learn from Eric. Mr. Merit understands that PMI is an evidence-based practice, and he believes it may benefit Eric and his peers by teaching a few of Eric's classmates how to engage him in social interaction.

When starting PMI, it is important to consider (a) the interpersonal skills of the participating peers, (b) the social communication and language skills of the student with ASD, and (c) instructional strategies peers can learn and use to address the social communication needs of the target student with ASD. In their study of PMI during recess, Harper and colleagues chose peers in the same class as the focus student with ASD, who demonstrated "excellent social and communication skills, and a history of volunteering to help" (Harper, Symon, & Frea, 2008 p. 818). In addition to positive social skills, Theimann and Goldstein (2004) considered peer status based on sociometric ratings when selecting peers. Other considerations include regular attendance, ability to engage in an activity for at least 10 minutes, and former positive interactions with the focus student with ASD (Sperry et al., 2010). To promote generalization, training multiple peers is optimal (Sperry et al., 2010). For example, Laushey and Heflin (2000) trained all of the classmates of a student with ASD in an inclusive setting, and rotated peer buddies daily.

The purpose of PMI is to improve the social communication of the learner with ASD; when implementing PMI, the characteristics and needs of the student with ASD must be considered. Relevant factors to the selection of strategies peers may implement include the child's language use, behaviors that may interfere with a successful social interaction, IEP goals, and skills important to families and teachers (Theimann & Kamps, 2008). In addition, strategies should target the social communication needs of the student with ASD. Skills may range by age and include play and sharing for young children, and focus more on interaction and maintaining communication as students enter school (Sperry et al., 2010). Studies using PMI have addressed a variety of skills that students with ASD have difficulty developing including joint attention, initiating and sustaining an interaction, taking turns, sharing, showing affection, as well as improving academics (Chan et al., 2009).

After reading about PMI, Mr. Merit decided to start a PMI approach similar to a method he found in his research (Harper et al., 2008; Pierce & Schreibman, 1995; Theimann & Goldstein, 2004). Mr. Merit wanted to see if PMI could help Eric engage in and maintain a conversation. Mr. Merit planned to observe the frequency of Eric's initiations and responses toward his peers at lunch. He selected six peers from the class who demonstrated positive prosocial behaviors, were considered well liked by their peers, and were often observed supporting their peers. He decided to invite a pair of peers to lunch each day for a week to see how Eric socially initiated and responded. Mr. Merit had games available that required turn taking. Throughout the week, Mr. Merit noted that Eric responded when his peers asked him questions, but he never attempted to engage his peers. As a result, Eric's peers typically stopped asking him questions after the first couple of minutes of lunch and began talking to each other. When playing a game, Eric would occasionally say, "my turn," but did not seem to direct the comment toward his peers. Eric took turns while playing and occasionally smiled. When playing Jenga, Eric laughed when all of the blocks fell. Mr. Merit decided to train the peers on how to encourage Eric to initiate and maintain a conversation during lunch.

When training peers to implement PMI, researchers typically teach strategies directly to encourage social interaction using modeling and practice with feedback (Chan et al., 2009). During training, the purpose of PMI is discussed, and multiple strategies that facilitate interaction are taught one at a time (Goldstein, Schneider, & Thiemann, 2007). After each strategy is taught, peers explain the strategy and how to use it, and then practice the skill, often by role-playing the strategy with an adult. Peers then begin using the strategies when interacting with students with ASD in authentic, natural settings as the adult provides prompts (e.g., direct verbal prompts, visual cues, gestures) and reinforcement as needed. Prompts and reinforcement are typically needed initially, but a plan should be in place to fade these supports as the interaction becomes more natural and intrinsically reinforcing (Goldstein et al., 2007). Strategies that appear to elicit greater social communication from students with ASD include gaining peer attention, making descriptive comments, requesting information, and acknowledging attempts made by students with ASD (Goldstein et al., 2007).

For example, Theimann and Goldstein (2004) taught elementary-age peers strategies to initiate (e.g., "say something nice"; "start talking"), maintain a social interaction (e.g., "keep talking"), and encourage a social initiation (e.g., "look, wait, and listen") from the child with ASD during a social activity. Similarly, Harper and colleagues (2008) taught third-grade general education peers to (a) gain the attention of their peer with ASD, (b) vary play activities, (c) narrate their play by commenting and describing the activity while playing, (d) reinforce attempts made by children with ASD to engage in play, and (e) offer the child with ASD a turn (Harper et al., 2008).

Mr. Merit chose five strategies from his research that encourage students with ASD to initiate and maintain conversation, including (1) getting attention, (2) talking through play, (3) eliciting communication, (4) offering a choice, and (5) talking to your friend. See Table 7-1 for a description and example of strategies found throughout the research literature on social skills (e.g., Harper, Symon, & Frea, 2008; Pierce & Schreibman, 1995; Thiemann & Goldstein, 2004).

Mr. Merit decided to complete the trainings over a week period during recess, and instruction lasted 20 minutes. In each session, the peers learned one of the strategies. Mr. Merit role-played each strategy while playing a game with the students. The peers then explained the strategy in their own words, and described how they would apply the strategy when playing the game with Eric. Next, the peers role-played the strategy with Mr. Merit as he used little social communication. Mr. Merit provided feedback after each student practiced the skill. If necessary, Mr. Merit asked students to role-play again after he provided feedback. In each session, Mr. Merit made sure that the games used would be available when the peers ate lunch with Eric. While the peers received training, they did not eat lunch with Eric because Mr. Merit wanted to wait and monitor Eric's progress once they completed the training.

At least initially, teacher prompting, positive reinforcement, and careful structuring of the environment may be necessary (Goldstein et al., 2007). Prompts may be (a) verbal (e.g., "Ask Eric what game he wants to play." "Remember to keep talking to your friend."), (b) picture cues (e.g., a picture of a child offering another child a choice of a game to play; a picture of a child talking to another child while playing a game), or (c) gestures (e.g., pointing to the game to indicate it is time to play). PMI should be part of a classroom routine and there should be time allowed for children with ASD to interact with their peers throughout the school day to encourage generalization (Sperry et al., 2010).

Table 7-1

Strategies for Initiating and Maintaining Attention	
Strategy	**Description and Example**
Getting Attention	Making sure the child with ASD is attending. *Mr. Merit taught peers to get Eric's attention before talking to him by calling his name, or saying "Eric, look...."*
Talking Through Play	Modeling play by verbally describing the play behavior and providing scripts. *Mr. Merit taught peers to make comments about the games (e.g., Great move! You got it!"), and narrate the activity (e.g., When playing Jenga, "I think it may be safer to take a block from the middle." "Uh oh, the tower is starting to wobble."*
Eliciting Communication	Teach the peer to look expectantly at the child with ASD, and wait for an initiation. *Mr. Merit taught peers to look at Eric before taking a turn and wait for a verbal or gestural reminder – "Your turn" or handing the peer the dice. Mr. Merit also taught peers to withhold an item Eric needed to proceed in a game or activity, and look at him and wait for an initiation.*
Offering a Choice	Present the child with ASD a choice of activity/game. *Mr. Merit taught peers to offer Eric a choice of game to play, and materials needed for the game (e.g., color of game piece, who will go first)*
Talking to Your Friend	Asking and answering questions, and following up on responses. *Mr. Merit taught peers to ask Eric questions about his likes and dislikes during lunch and game play ("What is your favorite movie?" "What do you like to do on the weekends?"). He also taught peers to follow up on Eric's responses ("What movies do you want to see?"; "That's cool, I like to play video games too. My favorite is. . .).*

Once Eric and his peers began eating lunch together, Mr. Merit provided stickers to indicate appropriate playing and using verbal cues as needed. As soon as the peers began to use these methods independently, Mr. Merit stopped prompting and moved further away from Eric and his peers. At the end of the lunch session, students were rewarded with an item from a treasure box if they earned at least three stickers. Mr. Merit created a checklist so he could document (check off) the strategies he observed the peers using during lunch with Eric. In addition, Mr. Merit monitored Eric's progress by counting how often Eric initiated a conversation or play with his peers. Mr. Merit also documented how often Eric and his peers maintained a conversation. That is, he recorded how many interactions extended beyond an initiation-response sequence. Eric began initiating after the first week and Mr. Merit faded the reinforcement. Mr. Merit checked in with the peers weekly, and found that they enjoyed playing games with Eric! Mr. Merit immediately began planning ways to get Eric's new friends to apply the strategies during recess and to encourage Eric to join them in the lunchroom.

Research suggests that following interventions using PMI, students with ASD improve social communication (Chan et al., 2009; Odom, Brown, et al., 2010; Reichow & Volkmar, 2010; Wang et al., 2011), but for some students with ASD, PMI that only includes peer training may not be sufficient (Goldstein et al., 2007). Providing training for peers along with systematic, direct social skill instruction for students with ASD can lead to greater and more sustainable gains (Goldstein et al., 2007). For example, scripts is one method used to directly teach social communication (Earles-Vollrath, Cook, Robbins, & Ben-Arieh, 2008). Scripts provide a way for students with ASD to initiate a reciprocal interaction with their general education peers (Goldstein et al., 2007). Another method that teaches individuals with ASD to actively participate in a social interaction with their peers is video modeling.

Video Modeling

Consistent with Bandura's (1969) social learning theory, video modeling is a flexible intervention that relies on the strength of observational learning. When participating in a video modeling intervention, a student watches videos of adults, peers, or himself or herself performing a target behavior. After viewing the video the student has an opportunity to use the targeted skill in a relevant context. Research has demonstrated the effectiveness of video modeling with neurotypical individuals and individuals with a variety of diagnoses (see Dowrick, 1999; Hitchcock, Dowrick, & Prater, 2003 for reviews). In recent years researchers have examined the use of video modeling with people with ASD and found it to be effective in increasing communication, social interaction, and daily living skills. In fact, video modeling is now considered an evidence-based practice for teaching individuals with ASD (National Professional Development Center on Autism Spectrum Disorders, 2009).

Why Is Video Modeling a Good Choice for Teaching Social Skills to Learners With ASD?

Though there is not a specific way to determine which students will respond to video modeling, there are several reasons why video modeling may be effective with individuals on the autism spectrum. First, people with autism typically display strengths in processing visual stimuli (Nikopoulos & Keenan, 2006). Delivering instruction through video capitalizes on this strength and watching videos may be a preferred activity for some people with ASD. Second, people with ASD may have overselective attention and have difficulty focusing on relevant cues (Rosenblatt, Bloom, & Koegel, 1995). Videos can be designed to highlight salient cues, and through the editing process irrelevant stimuli can be removed (Bellini, 2008).

Additionally, though learners on the autism spectrum frequently experience difficulty with generalization of skills, research suggests video modeling promotes generalization and maintenance of social skills (Bellini & Akullian, 2007; Delano, 2007). As a matter of fact, video modeling may produce more rapid acquisition and greater generalization than in vivo modeling (Charlop-Christy, Le, & Freeman, 2000). Finally, video modeling does not involve social demands of the learner during instruction. This factor may reduce anxiety and stress around learning (Bellini, 2008).

There are also a number of reasons that teachers may find video modeling a preferable method for teaching social skills. First, this is one of the few evidence-based interventions for teaching social skills to learners with ASD. Also, video modeling has been associated with increasing a variety of social skills including (a) spontaneous requesting (Wert & Neisworth, 2003), (b) social initiations and language production (Buggey, 2005), (c) conversational speech (Buggey, Toombs, Gardener, & Cervetti, 1999; Charlop & Milstein, 1989; Sherer et al., 2001), (d) the duration of appropriate play (Nikopoulous & Keenan, 2003, 2004), (e) verbal statements about play (D'Ateno et al., 2003; Taylor et al., 1999), and (f) compliment giving (Apple, Billingsley, & Schwartz, 2005). In short, video modeling improves the quantity and quality of social interaction. New technology has made the process of making videos relatively easy and implementing video modeling requires just a few minutes per day. After the video is created, instruction is delivered via video, procedures remain consistent, and classroom support staff without expertise in modeling and prompting procedures can implement the intervention with fidelity. The effectiveness and practicality of this intervention makes it a good choice for teachers of students with ASD.

Types of Video Modeling

There are four types of video modeling procedures: video self-modeling, basic video modeling, point-of-view video modeling, and video prompting (Cox, Delano, Sturgill, Franczone, & Collet-Klinberg, 2009). Following is a brief description of each procedure.

First, basic video modeling is the most common form of video modeling. A teacher writes a script for a video. A task analysis is often used to plan the script and peers may provide suggestions about the language that is incorporated into the script. The teacher then films a brief video (typically less than 5 minutes) in which peers or adults follow the script to illustrate performance of the target skill. The student watches the video prior to the teaching session. Thus the learner sees the skill being performed before entering a situation in which he or she will need to perform the skill.

Second, as the name implies, video self-modeling involves the learner watching videos of himself or herself performing the targeted skill (i.e., initiating). Video self-modeling consists of two strategies: positive self-review and video feedforward. When using positive self-review, the individual watches his or her "best" performance of a target skill that has already been learned (Buggey, 2009). The teacher removes any errors from the video during editing and prior to viewing. This form of video self-modeling is useful for increasing the rate of low-frequency behavior, building fluency in skills that are already within the learner's repertoire, and supporting generalization (Buggey, 2009). In contrast, video feedforward enables individuals to view themselves as they may perform in the future (Buggey, 2009). In other words, the teacher carefully crafts a video in which it appears that the learner is performing a skill that is just a little beyond her current performance. For example, if a child is using one-word utterances, the teacher may use video editing to make clips of individual words. Then the teacher would combine the clips into short phrases (i.e., 2 to 3 words) so that it appears that the learner is producing longer utterances (Buggey, 2009). In addition to teaching skills that are slightly beyond the individual's current level of performance, video feedforward may support generalization if teachers use videos that show the learner exhibiting the target skill in a new setting or with new communication partners. Finally, video feedforward is especially useful when the learner can perform individual components of a chained task or routine, but is not performing the whole task in the correct sequence (Bellini, 2008).

Initially, teachers may find it challenging to determine how to capture video clips of the student performing the target skill. However, Buggey (2009) suggests several simple ways to develop a video self-modeling tape. Role playing is appropriate for students who can follow directions and act out a script. Much like the procedure used in basic video modeling, the teacher prompts the student to act out the script. A second option is to have the student imitate an adult or peer. The camera is pointed at the student while the adult or peer provides prompts to help the student demonstrate correct performance of the target behavior. During editing, the teacher removes the prompts so that the final video shows the student performing the behavior independently. A final option for obtaining video, is to tape the student over a period of time to capture examples of the target behavior. Teachers using this procedure may need to have more experience in video editing and may need to spend more time filming.

Finally, two other forms of video modeling are video prompting and point-of-view video modeling. Video prompting is a strategy teachers use to teach students a chained task or routine. The teacher shows the student a video clip of the first step of a task analysis and then provides the student with an opportunity to perform the step. The teacher may give additional prompts if the student does not complete the step correctly. The student then watches a clip of the second step and has an opportunity to complete the second step. This process continues until each step of the task is completed. Some students may use video prompting procedures independently to complete tasks without teacher assistance.

Point-of-view video modeling is a unique strategy in which the student performing the task is not shown on camera. Instead, the video displays what the student would see when performing the target skill. Two studies (Hine & Wolery, 2006; Tetreault & Lerman, 2010) with promising results investigated this form of video modeling to teach social skills with participants demonstrating some gains.

Implementing Video Modeling

Video modeling is an evidence-based practice that has the potential of helping individuals with autism acquire, use, and generalize social skills. Table 7-2 provides an overview of the steps to follow when implementing video modeling. Similar sequences of procedural steps can be found elsewhere in the literature (e.g., Buggey, 2009). The resources listed at the end of the chapter will provide educators more detailed instructions for creating video modeling tapes and implementing the process.

Conclusion

Improving social functioning is perhaps the most critical intervention goal for students on the autism spectrum. Thus, it is important that students have ample instructional time devoted to social skills instruction in natural settings (Gresham, Sugai, & Horner, 2001) with their peers. It is also essential that educators implement social skills interventions that are most likely to benefit students. Peer-mediated interventions and video modeling are two such strategies.

Table 7-2

The Process of Using Video Modeling in Practice
Planning for Video Modeling
Identify the target skill
Develop a data collection procedure for monitoring progress
Collect baseline data on the target skill
Write a measurable learning objective
Select a form of video modeling
Obtain consent from parents or guardians prior to filming students
If applicable, identify other teaching strategies that will be implemented with video modeling to support the learner's progress on the objective (e.g., response prompting, reinforcement, visual supports)
Determine a schedule and procedure for viewing the video and collecting data
Identify how the video will be faded and plan for generalization across people, activities and locations
Creating the Video
Obtain the necessary equipment
Select a method to obtain examples of the target behavior on tape (e.g., role play, imitation, natural clips)
Write a script/task analysis
Train the models
Film and edit the video
Implementing Video Modeling
The student watches the video according to the planned schedule
Collect data on the student's behavior during video viewing (e.g., attending behavior)
Collect intervention data on the student's use of the target behavior
Make data-based modifications as needed
Fade the video and follow the plan for generalization

References

Apple, A., Billingsley, F., & Schwartz, I. (2005). Effects of video modeling alone and with self-management on compliment-giving behaviors of children with high functioning ASD. *Journal of Positive Behavior Interventions, 7,* 33-46.

Bandura, A. (1969). *Principles of behavior modification.* New York, NY: Holt Rinehart and Winston.

Bellini, S. (2008). *Building social relationships: A systematic approach to teaching social skills to children and adolescents with autism spectrum disorders and other social difficulties.* Shawnee Mission, KS: AAPC.

Bellini, S., & Akullian, J. (2007). A meta-analysis of video modeling and video self-modeling interventions for children and adolescents with autism spectrum disorders. *Exceptional Children, 73,* 261-284.

Bellini, S., Peters, J. K., Benner, L., & Hopf, A. (2007). A meta-analysis of school-based social skills interventions for children with autism spectrum disorders. *Remedial and Special Education, 28,* 153-162.

Buggey, T. (2005). Video modeling applications with students with autism spectrum disorder in a small private school setting. *Focus on Autism and Other Developmental Disabilities, 20,* 52-63.

Buggey, T. (2009). *Seeing is believing: Video self-modeling for people with autism and other developmental disabilities.* Bethesda, MD: Woodbine House.

Buggey, T., Toombs, K., Gardener, P., & Cervetti, M. (1999). Training responding behaviors in students with autism: Using VSM. *Journal of Positive Behavior Interventions, 1,* 205-214.

Chan, J. M., Lang, R., Rispoli, M., O'Reilly, M., Sigafoos, J., & Cole, H. (2009). Use of peer-mediated interventions in the treatment of autism spectrum disorders: A systematic review. *Research in Autism Spectrum Disorders, 3,* 876-889.

Charlop-Christy, M., Le, L., & Freeman, K. (2000). A comparison of video modeling and in vivo modeling for teaching children with autism. *Journal of Autism and Developmental Disorders, 30,* 537-552.

Charlop, M., & Milstein, J. (1989). Teaching autistic children conversational speech using video modeling. *Journal of Applied Behavior Analysis, 22,* 275-285.

Cox, A. W., Delano, M. E., Sturgill, T. R., Franzone, E., & Collet-Klinberg, L. (2009). *Video modeling-training materials*. Chapel Hill, NC: National Professional Development Center on Autism Spectrum Disorders, Frank Porter Graham Child Development Institute, University of North Carolina.

D'Ateno, P., Mangiapanello, K., & Taylor, B. (2003). Using video modeling to teach complex play sequences to a preschooler with autism. *Journal of Positive Behavior Interventions, 5,* 5-11.

Delano, M. E. (2007). Video modeling interventions for individuals with autism. *Remedial and Special Education, 28,* 33-42.

Dowrick, P. W. (1999). A review of self-modeling and related interventions. *Applied and Preventive Psychology, 8,* 23–39.

Earles-Vollrath, T. L., Cook, K. T., Robbins, L., & Ben-Arieh, J. (2008). Instructional strategies to facilitate successful learning outcomes for students with autism spectrum disorders. In R. L. Simpson & B. S. Myles (Eds.), *Educating children and youth with autism: Strategies for effective practice* (2nd ed., pp. 222-243). Austin, TX: Pro-Ed.

Goldstein, H., Schneider, N., & Thiemann, K. (2007). Peer-mediated social communication intervention: When clinical expertise informs treatment development and evaluation. *Topics in Language Disorders, 27,* 182-199.

Gresham, F. M., Sugai, G., & Horner, R. H. (2001). Interpreting outcomes of social skills training for students with high-incidence disabilities. *Exceptional Children, 67,* 331-344.

Harper, C. B., Symon, J. B., & Frea, W. D. (2008). Recess is time-in: Using peers to improve social skills of children with autism. *Journal of Autism and Developmental Disabilities, 38,* 815-826.

Hine, J., & Wolery, M. (2006). Using point-of-view video modeling to teach play to preschoolers with autism. *Topics in Early Childhood Special Education, 26,* 83-93.

Hitchcock, C., Dowrick, P., & Prater, M. (2003). Video self-modeling intervention in school based settings: A review. *Remedial and Special Education, 24,* 36-45.

Laushey, K. M., & Heflin, L. J. (2000). Enhancing social skills of kindergarten children with autism through the training of multiple peers as tutors. *Journal of Autism and Developmental Disorders, 30,* 183-193.

Loveland, K. A., & Tunali-Kotoski, B. (2005). *The school-age child with an autistic spectrum disorder.* In F. R. Volkmar, R. Paul, A, Klin, & D, Cohen (Eds.), *Handbook of autism and pervasive developmental disorders* (3rd ed., pp. 247-287). New York, NY: John Wiley & Sons.

Marans, W. D., Rubin, E., & Laurent, A., (2005). Addressing social communication skills in individuals with high-functioning autism and Asperger syndrome: Critical priorities in educational programming. In F. R. Volkmar, P. Rhea, A. Klin, & D. Cohen (Eds.), *Handbook of autism and pervasive developmental disorders* (3rd ed., pp. 977-1003). New York, NY: John Wiley & Sons.

National Professional Development Center on Autism Spectrum Disorders. (2009). *Evidence-based practices for children and youth with ASD.* Chapel Hill, NC: National Professional Development Center on Autism Spectrum Disorders, Frank Porter Graham Child Development Institute, University of North Carolina.

Nikopoulos, C., & Keenan, M. (2003). Promoting social initiations in children with autism using video modeling. *Behavioral Interventions, 18,* 87-108.

Nikopoulos, C., & Keenan, M. (2004). Effects of social initiations by children with autism. *Journal of Applied Behavior Analysis, 37,* 93-96.

Nikopoulos, C., & Keenan, M. (2006). *Video modeling and behavior analysis: A guide for teaching social skills to children with autism.* Philadelphia, PA: Jessica Kingsley.

Odom, S. L., Brown, W. H., Frey, T., Karasu, N., Smith-Canter, L. L., & Strain, P. S. (2010). Evidence-based practices for young children with autism: Contributions for single-subject design research. *Focus on Autism and Other Developmental Disabilities 18,* 166-175.

Odom, S. L., Collet-Klingenberg, L., Rogers, S. J., & Hatton, D. D. (2010). Evidence-based practices in interventions for children and youth with autism spectrum disorders. *Preventing School Failure, 54,* 275-282.

Olley, J. G. (2005). Curriculum and classroom structure. In F.R. Volkmar, P. Rhea, A. Klin, & D. Cohen (Eds.), *Handbook of autism and pervasive developmental disorders* (3rd ed., pp. 863-881). New York, NY: John Wiley & Sons.

Pierce, K., & Schreibman, L. (1995). Increasing complex social behaviors in children with autism: Effects of peer-implemented pivotal response training. *Journal of Applied Behavior Analysis, 28,* 285–295.

Reichow, B., & Volkmar, F. R. (2010). Social skills interventions for individuals with autism: Evaluation for evidence based practices within a best evidence synthesis framework. *Journal of Autism and Developmental Disabilities, 40,* 149-166.

Rosenblatt, J., Bloom, P., & Koegel, R. (1995). Overselective responding: Description, implications, and intervention. In R. Koegel & L. Koegel (Eds.), *Teaching children with autism: Strategies for initiating positive interactions and improving learning opportunities* (pp. 33-42). Baltimore, MD: Brookes.

Sherer, M., Pierce, K., Paredes, S., Kisacky, K., Ingersoll, B., & Schreibman, L. (2001). Enhancing conversation skills in children with autism via video technology: Which is better: "Self" or "other" as model? *Behavior Modification, 25,* 140-158.

Sperry, L., Neitzel, J., & Engelhardt-Wells. (2010). Peer-mediated instruction and intervention strategies for students with autism spectrum disorder. *Preventing School Failure, 54,* 256-264.

Taylor, B., Leven, L., & Jasper, S. (1999). Increasing play related statements in children with autism toward their siblings: Effects of video modeling. *Journal of Developmental and Physical Disabilities, 11,* 253-264.

Tetreault, A., & Lerman, D. (2010). Teaching social skills to children with autism using point-of-view video modeling. *Education and Treatment of Children, 33,* 395-419.

Thiemann, K., & Goldstein, H. (2004). Effects of peer training and written-text cueing on social communication of school-age children with pervasive developmental disorder. *Journal of Speech, Language, and Hearing Research, 47,* 126-144.

Thiemann, K., & Kamps, D. (2008). Promoting social-communicative competence of children with autism in integrated environments. In R. L. Simpson & B. S. Myles (Eds.), *Educating children and youth with autism: Strategies for effective practice* (2nd ed., pp. 267-298). Austin, TX: Pro-Ed.

Wang, S., Cui, Y., & Parrila, R. (2011). Examining the effectiveness of peer-mediated and video-modeling social skills interventions for children with autism spectrum disorders: A meta-analysis in single-case research using HLM. *Research in Autism Spectrum Disorders, 5,* 562-569.

Wert, B. Y., & Neisworth, J. T. (2003). Effects of video self-modeling on spontaneous requesting in children with autism. *Journal of Positive Behavior Interventions, 5,* 30-34.

Additional Resources by Topic

Peer-Mediated Instruction

Carter, E., Cushing, L., & Kennedy, C. (2009). *Peer support strategies for improving all students' social lives and learning.* Baltimore, MD: Brookes.

Janney, R., & Snell, M. E. (2006). *Social relationships and peer support.* Baltimore, MD: Brookes.

Video Modeling

Buggey, T. (2009). *Seeing is believing: Video self-modeling for people with autism and other developmental disabilities.* Bethesda, MD: Woodbine House.

Nikopoulos, C., & Keenan, M. (2006). *Video modeling and behavior analysis: A guide for teaching social skills to children with autism.* Philadelphia, PA: Jessica Kingsley.

Social Skills

Bellini, S. (2008). *Building social relationships: A systematic approach to teaching social skills to children and adolescents with autism spectrum disorders and other social difficulties.* Shawnee Mission, KS: AAPC.

Effective Toilet Training

Martha E. Snell and Monica E. Delano

Learning to use the toilet is one of the most difficult self-care skills to teach because it requires a functional bladder, an awareness of bladder fullness and bowel tension, and many related dressing and grooming skills. Most children, including those with disabilities, master bowel control before bladder control and daytime before nighttime dryness. Children with disabilities, including autism spectrum disorders (ASD), frequently experience delays in learning these skills. Because incontinence can have a damaging effect on the individual, can be stressful for families, and is more difficult to eliminate in older students, it is important that teachers know effective toilet training strategies.

Definition of Toilet Training

Target Skills

This chapter addresses instruction of bladder regulation or self-initiation during the daytime. Readers are referred to Snell and Delano (2011) for in-depth coverage. Two types of toilet training skill objectives that educational teams should identify are (a) elimination and (b) related grooming skills. Elimination objectives span from (a) being regulated or habit trained (student learns to go when taken to the toilet and to remain dry during other times), to (b) self-initiation (student learns the natural cues of bladder fullness and to request the toilet or simply to go), to (c) independence (student learns to toilet without assistance). Related grooming skills include getting to the toilet, clothing manipulation, wiping and flushing, and hand washing. Elimination objectives are selected based on toileting records, whereas related skills are selected after gathering observation data.

Barry eliminates when taken but needs to learn to self-initiate, to get to and from the toilet, to push down and pull up his pants, and to flush when finished. Hand washing will wait until later.

Prerequisites and Assessment

Students are ready for toilet training if they (a) have a stable and not random pattern of elimination, (b) daily periods of being dry (1-2 hours), and (c) are age 2 or older. A baseline toileting record should be kept on a grid of days by 15- or 30-minute time intervals. Although these shorter intervals demand more staff time, they provide a more accurate picture of the student's elimination pattern. This information helps determine if students meet the first two criteria; if a traditional method is selected it is crucial to know when the child typically has a full bladder. Teams need to develop a good task analysis (see Chapter 4 on Systematic Instruction) that reflects day-to-day conditions and the sequence of toileting skills that are likely to be targeted for a student. The task analysis is used to guide a baseline assessment observation; teachers may use single opportunity assessment (stop after the first error and score all remaining task steps as incorrect) or multiple opportunity assessment (perform any missed steps for the student so that every step can be assessed). A single-opportunity task analytic assessment is fast and teaching can start right after the first error, but it does not give assessment information for each task step. Assessment results are summarized as number of steps independently performed. After instruction begins, the same assessment approach is repeated periodically to evaluate the student's learning.

For younger children, assessment of elimination can be made more accurate by using *dry-pants checks*. This method can also be used during teaching to determine if students are wet and need changing or if they are dry and need positive reinforcement. Dry-pants checks are done in private unless the child is very young or the setting is isolated. All team members should use the same procedure which starts by telling the student that you are going to check to see if he or she has dry pants. Then place the student's hand in yours and together gently check the outside and then the inside of the pants to assess their condition (Anderson, Jablonski, Thomeer, & Knapp, 2007, p. 131). With small children, the toddler-training diapers with wetness sensors may be used in place of feeling the pants. If the student is dry, praise him or her for being dry and record the performance on the data sheet. When the pants are wet, tell the student in a neutral tone that he or she is wet and record this performance. Immediately change the student and return to the previous activity. When children are changed to dry pants, it is healthier for the student if adults don't confuse recent accidents with earlier accidents.

In the general education classroom, peers may become aware that a classmate is being assessed or toilet trained because of the frequency of removing the child to a nearby bathroom to check for dryness. If such issues arise, the team should handle them with care and perhaps as part of peer support efforts (Snell & Janney, 2005). The team must be sensitive to the student's right to privacy when selecting the location for baseline assessment and training. Toileting records should be easily accessible by team members, but still be secure and private.

Teams may decide to postpone instruction on wiping or going to and leaving the toilet and instead prompt them through these steps without the goal of independence; in such cases these steps are listed on the task analysis as *teacher steps*. Putting all of the steps, including any teacher steps, on the task analysis data sheet helps keep staff consistent. Steps that are more difficult for a student (e.g., latching a stall door, undoing and redoing pants fasteners, wiping, and hand washing) can be adapted or added to the task analysis after the student is successful with the basic steps. For example, with younger children, a good method of teaching wiping requires the child to stand up and then wipe rather than to remain seated; older students will sit and may learn to use premoistened wipes for easier cleansing (Stokes, Cameron, Dorsey, & Fleming, 2004).

Implementation of Toilet Training

There are three broad approaches to toilet training students with autism. The emphasis with all methods is on reinforcing students for eliminating in the toilet and for remaining dry. The main differences among the approaches are the toileting schedule and the intensity of training (Snell & Delano, 2011).

1. *Traditional methods* are more "natural" but potentially slower and with more errors. They rely on toileting students at the time when the bladder is naturally full. These times are identified from elimination records (Baker & Brightman, 1997).

2. *Systematic schedule training* involves the addition of one or more procedures associated with intensive methods (e.g., access to fluids, underpants not diapers, dry-pants checks) and increased regular toileting.

3. *Intensive methods* require (a) access to fluids in order to create more frequent bladder tension; (b) dry-pants checks; (c) increased training time each day; (d) long periods in the bathroom; and (e) may include accident interruption, moisture-signaling devices, and request training. Consequences for accidents vary from neutral to negative (Anderson et al., 2007).

Issues to Resolve Prior to Training

Before planning the training program and regardless of what approach is selected, the team must address two issues. The first issue is whether the student will wear diapers or underpants during training. Clothing students in training pants or ordinary underwear has several advantages: accidents can be more quickly and accurately detected, the pants-down-and-up maneuvers are easier, and student can experience the naturally unpleasant feedback from wet clothing that disposable diapers have virtually eliminated. The difficulty with having students wear underpants is that their accidents can be noticed by peers and be stigmatizing, especially beyond the preschool years. Teams (including family members) must decide the appropriateness of having students wear diapers; teams may make exceptions to the no-diapers guideline with older students to avoid noticeable accidents. Training pants with disposable diapers over them may allow the student both privacy and feedback, although removal for toileting will likely require assistance. If intensive methods are used or if training occurs in an isolated location or at home during the summer it is best to have students wear training pants.

The second issue involves identifying methods of communication and visual cues (gestures, photos, picture symbols) that are effective with the student. When taking a student for a scheduled trip to the toilet, start by adding a toileting symbol to the student's picture or word schedule. For some students, Now–Next visual cues (first toilet, then computer), social narratives or Social Stories™ about toileting, and success charts can be valuable additions to the toileting approach that the team selects. Some researchers have reported better success when students view short toileting videos before every toileting opportunity, coupled with systematic instruction, than with only systematic instruction (Keen, Brannigan, & Cuskelly, 2007).

Traditional Approach

Traditional toilet training involves taking a child to the toilet at regular intervals throughout the day or whenever the student shows signs of the need to toilet and praising him/her for any eliminations on the toilet and for remaining dry. These simple steps are successful for most typical students when they meet the prerequisites, however this approach should be systematized in the following ways to increase its success when students have disabilities (Anderson et al., 2007; Baker & Brightman, 1997; Schaefer & DiGeronimo, 1997):

1. Select a few regular toileting times (off or on the toilet) from the student's baseline elimination pattern. Add any logical times (e.g., arrival, following lunch, and before departure). These times become the scheduled occasions when students are taken to the toilet. Add more times with success. Follow this toileting schedule consistently, making adjustments only if the program is unsuccessful and then based on the student's elimination pattern.

2. For students who are neither bladder nor bowel trained, focus on bowel training first because it is easier to learn. Continue using diapers. Change wet pants in the bathroom using a neutral manner.

3. Work with parents to learn how a student signals the need to eliminate. Whenever these signals occur, even at nonscheduled times, take the student to the bathroom immediately, urging speed and restraint ("Quick, let's go to the toilet!"). Document these times on the student's record sheet.

4. Use the regular toilet, with adaptations added only as necessary. Be sure the student's feet are flat on the floor or on a nonslip support and that the student is sitting securely. Students who are unstable while sitting will have trouble relaxing the sphincters that control elimination.

5. Keep the toileting time positive but not distracting (e.g., keep unneeded conversation to a minimum; use rewarding activities beyond praise or brief reinforcers after toileting and out of the bathroom).

6. Take the student to the toilet about (a) 15 minutes before the scheduled time for bowel training, or (b) 5 to 10 minutes before the scheduled time(s) for bladder training. Determine the length of time for sitting on the basis of individual student characteristics. The student needs to sit on the toilet long enough to have the opportunity to eliminate, but not for so long that toileting becomes aversive. Never leave the student unsupervised.

7. Reinforce the student immediately when elimination occurs. If elimination does not occur, return the student to the classroom for a 5- to 10-minute interval and then return to the toilet. Continue alternating until elimination occurs. Record any extra toileting times and the outcomes so that the team can evaluate progress and adjust times as needed.

8. As the student is successful, consider extending the goals, adding more times or more related skills.

Systematic Schedule Approach

When more traditional approaches are insufficient, teachers may consider adding one or more additional procedures: (a) increased reinforcement for successes, (b) more frequent scheduled toileting with underpants instead of diapers, (c) dry-pants checks, (d) natural consequences for accidents, (e) free access to fluids, (f) use of moisture-signaling devices, or (g) transfer of stimulus control. Alternately teams can start by adding the first three procedures (a, b, and c) to a traditional method and by gradually lengthening the time between scheduled toileting opportunities (Anderson et al., 2007). Following are several variations.

More frequent regular toileting involves an increase in the number of times students are taken to the toilet without giving extra fluids (e.g., every hour, every half hour). When a student's baseline did not yield dependable periods of dryness over time and the student did not show progress with fewer target times, regularly increasing the number of toileting trips may help. However, when the team decides to increase toileting trips there is less time for instruction in other areas and time scheduled in general education classrooms is threatened. When regular toileting is the only change made to a traditional program that is not working, it may continue to be unsuccessful.

With a systematic approach the team should *individualize their strategies*: the specific length of time between dry-pants checks, their communication mode and vocabulary, the feedback given for wetness and dryness, and the reinforcement for continence. Always focus feedback toward increasing student awareness of being dry or wet; when wet, pants should be changed with little comment (simply, "You're wet," said in a neutral tone).

Teams will want to systematize the *consequences given to students for accidents*. When students are first learning, some accidents must be expected. Thus, a regular procedure for responding to accidents should be planned by the team. In many cases, planned ignoring is an appropriate strategy. The team may consider several options:

Extinction: Following an accident, change the student's pants and clean the student in a neutral manner, with little socialization. Avoid reinforcing activities too soon after accidents.

Mild disapproval: As soon as an accident is discovered, approach the student in a manner that respects privacy, have the student feel and look at the pants, and express some age-appropriate form of disapproval in your words and facial expressions. Change the student's pants as with the extinction procedure.

Cleanup: Use mild disapproval and require the student to participate in washing him or herself with a damp cloth and changing clothes. Student cleanup should be implemented as a natural consequence, with little socializing and with no punitive talk or handling. Use the cleanup participation strategy cautiously, as students who require prompting to clean themselves may be reinforced by the extra attention or by leaving classroom activities; some students may become upset emotionally.

Most experts and practitioners agree that it is the positive aspects of teaching, not the negative consequences, that lead to learning new skills.

Some teams will want to add *moisture-signaling devices* to help speed feedback to students. The toilet alert is built into a special toileting chair (for young students) or into a small toilet bowl that fits under the regular toilet seat and catches eliminations, triggering an auditory signal. The pants alert often involves clip-on devices that detect moisture when students eliminate in their clothing. These devices are available online (e.g., Wet-Stop®, Sears®, and JCPenney™); pediatricians can also direct parents or teachers to suppliers.

Despite the efficiency of signaling the moment of elimination, there are many disadvantages of moisture-signaling equipment in a toileting program (e.g., noise, its obviousness to others, expense, and breakage). Teams should view using moisture-signaling devices as an option in unusual situations in which toileting progress has been minimal; bladder control is important for the student; and training is more isolated, such as during a summer program or at home.

Video modeling with or without systematic instruction has been used in several toileting studies with children having autism.Bainbridge and Myles (1999) demonstrated the use of *priming* in which a student watches a 5-minute video of children learning to use the toilet. After each viewing of the video, the student was prompted to use the toilet. This approach, without additional training, resulted in increased self-initiations for toileting and dry diapers during checks, but not bladder control. (The video used in Bainbridge and Myles, 1999 was *It's Potty Time* by Howard, 1991.) Keen et al., (2007) reported that students who received intensive training and viewed video models made more progress than those receiving intensive training alone. Video modeling appears to be a promising teaching tool for students with autism who respond to visual cues (National Professional Development Center on Autism Spectrum Disorders, 2009).

Intensive Training Programs

Intensive methods are complex training packages based primarily on the research of Azrin and Foxx (1971); some intensive methods conflict with today's emphasis on positive interventions and they also have not been consistently replicated. Typically, intensive approaches have been used with students in nonschool or institutional settings and have employed one or more of the following questionable practices: (a) potentially dangerous fluid increases, (b) removal of the student from most instruction except toileting, (c) removal of the student from opportunities to participate with peers without disabilities, and (d) excessive punishment.

Several versions of intensive approaches do not use aversive methods: (a) Richmond, 1983; (b) Cicero & Pfadt, 2002, and Keen et al., 2007; and (c) Anderson et al., 2007, and

Chung, 2007. All or most of the following procedures were used by these researchers as part of the intensive intervention.

Graduated guidance and total task sequence
Positive reinforcement for successes
Free access to fluids
Underpants, no diapers, and limited clothing
Training in 30-minute cycles in the bathroom
Training session primarily in the bathroom
Dry pants checks
Initiation request training
Accident interruption and rush to toilet with praise for success
Accidents followed by brief reprimand and simple correction (assistance in cleanup)

Intensive toileting approaches should be used only with total team support and if other less intrusive methods do not work after being implemented accurately for a fair trial of time. Fortunately, if intensive methods are necessary, there are adequate effective and positive strategies from which teams can select; punitive intensive approaches should not be used.

The logic for increasing the student's fluid intake is to increase the opportunities to urinate and thus to be taught and obtain reinforcement. Increasing fluids to boost the quantity of bladder-training sessions must be accompanied by certain precautions so as not to disrupt the balance of electrolytes in the body. The decision to increase fluids requires the approval by the family doctor and should not be used with students on medications that increase urinary retention or those who have seizure disorders or hydrocephaly. It is especially important to talk with a doctor about the amount of fluid that is safe for the individual student as this will vary based upon size and underlying health issues. Drinks (e.g., water or decaffeinated, low-sugar beverages) should be accessible to students, but reinforcement should not be provided for drinking additional fluids.

Using an intensive approach should be avoided if possible. However, if the team has implemented several less intensive approaches and a thorough analysis of ongoing elimination data suggests a lack of progress, the use of an intensive approach may be warranted. These approaches are the most difficult to implement in a school setting, severely restrict the amount of time available for instruction in other skills, and make great demands on staff time. Therefore, it is important that the team individualize the program and design it so that implementation is feasible for staff.

Toileting can be a challenging skill to teach, but one that most students can learn using the procedures outlined in this chapter. Since incontinence hinders independence and has a harmful impact on the student, it is critical that teams persist in teaching toileting and related dressing and grooming skills. The following case study illustrates toilet training with a child named Barry.

Barry is a 4-year old with autism who still uses diapers. His educational team identified toileting as a high-priority goal because Barry will transition to kindergarten next year. His teachers and caregivers have been using traditional toilet training methods and Barry has not made sufficient progress. The team decided to make several modifications to Barry's toilet training program. First, they replaced diapers with training pants at school. This change would enable staff to respond quickly to accidents and allow Barry to experience the natural consequence of accidents. Barry's parents will continue using diapers in the evenings when they need to make dinner and help children with homework and baths. Second, the team increased the number of scheduled toileting opportunities and added dry-pants checks every 15 minutes across the school day. Finally, the team increased reinforcement (e.g., praise and access to preferred activity) for dryness and successful elimination. After implementing this program for 7 weeks, Barry demonstrated a reduction in accidents and eliminated 70% of the time when he was taken to the bathroom.

References

Anderson, S. R., Jablonski, A. L., Thomeer, M. L., & Knapp, V. M. (2007). *Self-help skills for people with autism: A systematic teaching approach.* Bethesda, MD: Woodbine House.

Azrin, N. H., & Foxx, R. M. (1971). A rapid method of toilet training and institutionalized retarded. *Journal of Applied Behavior Analysis, 4,* 89-99.

Bainbridge, N., & Myles, B. S. (1999). The use of priming to introduce toilet training to a child with autism. *Focus on Autism and Other Developmental Disabilities. 14,* 106-109.

Baker, B. L., & Brightman, A. J. (1997). *Steps to independence: Teaching everyday skills to children with special needs* (3rd ed.). Baltimore, MD: Paul H. Brookes.

Chung, K. (2007). Modified version of Azrin and Foxx's rapid toilet training. *Journal of Developmental and Physical Disabilities, 19,* 449-455.

Cicero, F. R., & Pfadt, A. (2002). Investigation of a reinforcement-based toilet training procedure for children with autism. *Research in Developmental Disabilities, 23,* 319-331.

Howard, B. J. (1991). It's potty time [videorecording]. *The Duke Family Series.* Dallas, TX: Learning Through Entertainment.

Keen, D., Brannigan, K. L., & Cuskelly, M. (2007). Toilet training for children with autism: The effects of video modeling. *Journal of Developmental and Physical Disabilities, 19,* 291-303.

National Professional Development Center on Autism Spectrum Disorders. (2009). *Evidence-based practices for children and youth with ASD.* Chapel Hill, NC: University of North Carolina.

Richmond, G. (1983). Shaping bladder and bowel continence in developmentally retarded preschool children. *Journal of Autism and Developmental Disorders, 13,* 197-205.

Schaefer, C. E., & DiGeronimo, T. F. (1997). *Toilet training without fear* (Rev. ed.). New York, NY: Signet Books.

Snell, M. E., & Delano, M. E. (2011). Teaching self-care skills. In M. E. Snell & F. Brown *Instruction of students with severe disabilities* (pp. 377-430). Upper Saddle River, NJ: Pearson Education.

Snell, M. E., & Janney, R. E. (2005). *Practices for inclusive schools: Collaborative teaming* (2nd ed.). Baltimore, MD: Paul H. Brookes.

Stokes, J.V., Cameron, M. J., Dorsey, M. F., & Fleming, E. (2004). Task analysis, correspondence training, and general case instruction for teaching personal hygiene skills. *Behavioral Interventions, 19,* 121-135.

Additional Resources

Anderson, S. R., Jablonski, A. L., Thomeer, M. L., & Knapp, V. M. (2007). *Self-help skills for people with autism: A systematic teaching approach.* Bethesda, MD: Woodbine House.

Coucouvanis, J. A. (2008). *The potty journey: Guide to toilet training children with special needs, including autism and related disorders.* Shawnee Mission, KS: Autism Asperger.

Snell, M. E., & Brown, F. (2011). *Instruction of students with severe disabilities* (7th ed.). Upper Saddle River, NJ: Pearson Education.

Section III

Access to the General Education Curriculum

Collaboration

Maureen Walsh and Darlene E. Perner

Teachers who instruct students with autism spectrum disorders (ASD) need to work closely together to share their understanding of its many features. It is imperative that teachers form this collaboration and come to agreement about their teaching approaches due to the complexity of the individual needs of these students (Kilham, 2009). Collaboration is a rewarding endeavor, but can often be difficult to achieve in an instructional setting.

Collaboration refers to two or more people working together toward a common goal. In the field of education, teachers collaborate in many ways. One particular type of collaboration that is receiving much attention is the co-teaching model (Friend & Cook, 2007). In this collaborative relationship, the general and special education teacher work together to instruct all students in an inclusive education classroom. It requires commitment and flexibility from both teachers. The collaborative process in a co-teaching model requires

1. self-reflection;
2. professional development;
3. shared decisions;
4. regularly scheduled meetings supporting open communication;
5. on-going assessments of students' strengths and needs, as well as assessments of instructional approaches and collaborative efforts; and
6. a maintained focus on the ultimate goal of meeting all students' needs.

Students with disabilities undoubtedly have the potential to benefit and prosper in an inclusive setting when a strong collaborative support system exists. Specifically, the partnership between the special and general education teacher is instrumental in the outcome of inclusive classroom experiences for students with and without disabilities. Yet this partnership often leads to challenges that can further complicate the task of providing meaningful inclusive educational experiences for all students. Therefore, it is essential that the partnering teachers recognize the preliminary work needed prior to embarking on this joint venture.

Preparing for the Collaboration Process

Step 1: Self-Reflection

It is vital that both teachers reflect on their own beliefs and attitudes toward inclusion. The first important question to be answered is, "Do I really think this can work?" Many general educators have uncertainties, possibly in response to feeling ill-prepared to teach students with disabilities (Gallagher, Malone, & Ladner, 2009) and many special educators may feel ill-prepared to teach core content or lack subject-area expertise. Administrators have the power to help diminish such fears by providing their teachers with proper training through professional development experiences. Participating in co-teaching seminars, observing co-teachers in action, and having a mentor with experience in co-teaching are three simple ways that may help to enhance the skills and confidence levels of teachers. Many teachers may find that they do have the knowledge and ability necessary to meet diverse needs.

Another potential reason for educators' skepticism about including students in the general education classroom is the notion that the "special education classroom" is a more suitable placement option for students with autism and other developmental disabilities. Students with disabilities do not necessarily, however, learn more in the special education classroom; they do as well or better when appropriate supports are provided in general education classrooms (Lawrence-Brown, 2004). Identifying appropriate supports and making them available to students is critical for successful inclusion (See Chapter 10, Differentiating Instruction). Coming to terms with this reality could have a positive impact on attitudes toward inclusion. Training in how to differentiate instruction and having opportunities to observe in high quality inclusive classrooms will also help teachers see that students with disabilities can thrive in general education classrooms. Having a positive attitude is the first step in helping to make inclusion successful for all students. There are a number of other questions that co-teaching partners should answer before engaging in this collaborative model (see Table 9-1). Once teachers recognize their own perspective on issues related to co-teaching, they will be ready to convey their position to their partner and begin collaborating with their colleague.

Table 9-1

Self-Reflection Questions	
What do I see as my strengths?	In which areas would I like to improve?
What are my views in relation to classroom management?	What are my views in relation to instructional approaches?
What are my views in relation to instructional planning?	What are my views in relation to grading procedures?
What are my views in relation to accommodations?	What are my views in relation to modifications?

Step 2: Sharing Perspectives and Developing a Cooperative Teaching Plan

While planning lessons that will be co-taught, teachers need to share their ideas and opinions on how best to implement a particular lesson that will meet the needs of all students. A cooperative teaching plan can help co-teachers communicate (a) their perspective about a lesson and clarify what they will teach, (b) how they will teach it, (c) what the specific tasks of each teacher will be during the lesson, (d) what method(s) will be used to assess students, and (e) what accommodations and/or modifications will be needed. Table 9-2 is a cooperative teacher plan to assist teachers in planning lessons together.

Step 3: Establishing the Ground Rules for Communication and Planning

Collaboration takes commitment. Like any partnered relationship there are ups and downs. Understanding that obstacles are probable and addressing them before difficulties arise is another proactive approach. Few people enjoy confrontation; nevertheless, agreeing to attend to issues head-on is one more positive method. It is important to schedule weekly meetings for the purpose of discussing the positives and negatives of teaching together. Even though these meetings may be awkward at first, they help to create a strong communicative relationship. Routine meetings for tackling issues are preferable to the alternative of confronting your co-teaching peer with those dreaded words, "We need to talk!" Laying the ground rules and identifying how to deal with difficult matters together is time well spent.

While discussing concerns it is important for co-teachers to remember that critical statements are not personal attacks; critically analyzing co-teaching situations is an important part of the process. Considering word choices, however, is crucial so that messages are not misconstrued or received as harsh. Keep an open-mind and when asking questions for clarification ask open-ended questions in order to elicit in-depth responses. It is important for teachers to understand each other's collaborative style and make adjustments to one's own, in order to provide what is needed to be successful co-teachers (Conderman, Johnston-Rodriguez, & Hartman, 2009). Compromise goes a long way.

As a pair, maintain perspective by remembering that collaboration is necessary to meet the needs of individuals with disabilities. The collaborative team is responsible for creating ways for students to meaningfully participate in lessons that would otherwise be inaccessible (Lawrence-Brown, 2004). The key is to promote lessons that actively engage all students. The challenge for co-teachers in an inclusive classroom is finding a balance between the curriculum standards and the individualized education program (IEP) goals for students with disabilities. When co-teachers choose to differentiate instruction they are likely to achieve that balance. Lessons that are differentiated can meet the varied instructional levels of students, promote active learning, and connect subject matter with student interests.

Table 9-2	
Cooperative Teaching Plan	
Lesson:	Lesson:
Date:	Date:
Core concepts and skills for this lesson	Core concepts and skills for this lesson
Co-teaching model(s)	Co-teaching model(s)
Specific tasks for the general education teacher	Specific tasks for the general education teacher
Specific tasks for the special education teacher	Specific tasks for the special education teacher
Method(s) to assess student performance	Method(s) to assess student performance
Accommodations and/or modifications	Accommodations and/or modifications

Reminder: Schedule a Weekly Meeting for Planning (at least one/week at consistent day/time)

Step 4: Selecting a Collaboration Model

Just as it is essential for both teachers to get to know each other, it is equally important for both teachers to get to know all of their students. Finding a balance among several approaches to co-teaching (lead and support, parallel teaching, station teaching, alternative teaching, and team teaching) allows teachers the capacity to work with all students (see Table 9-3). Unfortunately, many co-teaching pairs fall in the trap of using solely one co-teaching approach; they consistently rely on "lead and support" with the general education teacher in the lead role and the special education teacher in the supporting role. As a result, the general educator misses the chance to work closely with the students with autism and developmental disabilities and share his/her content area expertise; likewise the special educator fails to become further acquainted with the students without disabilities and provide effective instructional strategies.

When co-teachers use an array of differentiated instructional methods along with flexible cooperative grouping arrangements, they maximize the opportunity to assess students' needs, and instruct students individually and in small groups. Students, particularly students with autism, benefit from peer modeling and socialization when they are included in flexible grouping.

Step 5: Identifying Supports for Students

As co-teachers establish the needs of their students, they can plan accordingly. Following the premise of *universal design,* a rule of thumb for teachers is, "What may help one student will most likely help others." In other words, if teachers plan to devise a study guide for one student, they should make it available for all students. Others might need that study guide, but just as important, it reduces the stigma associated with being the one student receiving extra supports.

Summary

Although the collaborative process presents obstacles such as time constraints, there are numerous advantages to using a co-teaching approach. The co-teaching partnership can serve as a model for the students by highlighting mutual respect and cooperation. Two teachers have the advantage of two viewpoints, shared knowledge, and supported discipline (Gallagher, Malone, & Ladner, 2009). Furthermore, all students experience the sense of belonging as an alternative to segregation.

Including students with ASD in the general education setting can yield positive results for all students. Co-teachers have the power to make inclusion work as long as they remain focused on the ultimate goal of meeting all students' needs.

Table 9-3

Collaboration Models/Models of Co-Teaching	
Model	**Description**
Lead and Support	One teacher takes the lead with the lesson while the other teacher supports instruction by circulating around the classroom, monitoring all students, and assisting those needing help. It is important that the teachers switch roles, achieving a balance between lead and support. The disadvantage with this model is that if teachers do not regularly switch roles students perceive only one as an actual teacher and the other as a helper in the room.
Parallel Teaching	Both teachers are simultaneously teaching one-half of the class. The groups are heterogeneous. Teachers are teaching the same content through this model.
Station Teaching	This model is quite similar to parallel teaching, yet differs from parallel teaching in that the teachers divide the instructional content. Each teacher is responsible for teaching a portion of the content. After teaching to one group, the teachers exchange groups and teach their portion of the content to the second group.
Alternative Teaching	This model is used when a small group of students is in need of instruction in a way that is somehow different than the larger group. This is often used for reviewing or re-teaching. The disadvantage with this model is the possible stigma associated with being part of the small group.
Team Teaching	Both teachers are responsible for instruction and monitoring of all students. The teachers alternate roles in a fluid balanced manner. When teachers effectively execute this approach it is quite difficult for an observer to determine which teacher is the content area teacher and which one is the special educator.

References

Conderman, G., Johnston-Rodriguez, S., & Hartman, P. (2009). Communicating and collaborating in co-taught classrooms. *TEACHING Exceptional Children Plus, 5*(5) Article 3. Retrieved from http://escholarship.bc.edu/education/tecplus/vol5/iss5/art3

Friend, M., & Cook, L. (2007). *Interactions: Collaboration skills for school professionals* (5ᵗʰ ed.). Boston, MA: Allyn & Bacon.

Gallagher, P. A., Malone, D. M., & Ladner, J. R. (2009). Social-psychological support personnel: Attitudes and perceptions of teamwork supporting children with disabilities. *Journal of Social Work in Disability & Rehabilitation, 8,* 1-20.

Kilham, C. H. (2009). Online wiki collaboration by teachers of students with autism spectrum disorders. *Australasian Journal of Special Education, 33,* 117-129.

Lawrence-Brown, D. (2004). Differentiated instruction: Inclusive strategies for standards-based learning that benefit the whole class. *American Secondary Education, 32*(3), 34-62.

Additional Resources

Dukes, C., & Lamar-Dukes, P. (2009). Inclusion by design: Engineering inclusive practices in secondary schools. *TEACHING Exceptional Children, 41*(3), 16-23.

Friend, M. (2007). The coteaching partnership. *Educational Leadership, 64*(5), 48-52.

Friend, M. (2008). *Co-teach! A handbook for creating and sustaining effective classroom partnerships in inclusive schools.* Greensboro, NC: Marilyn Friend.

Friend, M., & Bursuck, W. D. (2009). *Including students with special needs: A practical guide for classroom teachers* (5ᵗʰ ed.). Columbus, OH: Merrill.

Friend, M., & Cook, L. (2010). *Interactions: Collaboration skills for school professionals* (6th ed.). Columbus: OH: Merrill.

Gargiulo, R. M., & Metcalf, D. (2010). *Teaching in today's inclusive classrooms: A universal design for learning approach.* Bemont, CA: Wadsworth.

Lingo, A. S., Barton-Arwood, S. M., & Jolivette, K. (2011). Teachers working together: Improving learning outcomes in the inclusive classroom – practical strategies and examples. *TEACHING Exceptional Children, 43*(3), 6-13.

Mastropieri, M. A., & Scruggs, T. E. (2010). *The inclusive classroom: Strategies for effective differentiated instruction* (4th ed.). Upper Saddle River, NJ: Merrill.

Internet Resources

http://www.powerof2.org/
This is an interactive resource designed to help teachers successfully include children with special needs into the general education classroom.

http://www.specialconnections.ku.edu/
This is the Special Connections web site at the University of Kansas (KU). The link to Collaboration provides topics, with detailed information and links to resources, on case studies, cooperative teaching including teacher tools, teams, and working effectively with paraeducators.

http://www.interventioncentral.com/
This web site provides a variety of academic and behavioral interventions that can assist the special and general education teacher in working together to provide instruction in inclusive classroom settings.

Differentiating Instruction Using Tiered Instruction

Darlene E. Perner and Maureen Walsh

In a way, it's just shaking up the classroom so it's a better fit for more kids.
Carol Ann Tomlinson (From an interview with Leslie J. Kiernan, 1996)

Differentiated instruction is a process that helps general and special education teachers collaborate and meet the diverse learning needs of all students in inclusive classrooms. Teachers should consider a number of important principles when creating a differentiated classroom. These principles can range from adjusting the *content* (the material being presented); the *process* (the methods and activities that help students understand the concepts or skills being taught); and the *product* (the artifacts that students produce to demonstrate their learning) to creating a positive, supportive classroom environment (Tomlinson, 1999). Differentiated instruction involves teachers and students helping each other in learning and in social contexts. Other principles include respecting students' abilities, providing meaningful tasks, giving students choices, and employing flexible grouping. In differentiated classrooms, teachers continuously assess students' abilities/background knowledge (*readiness*), interests, and learning preferences (*learning profile*) and use these data to adjust the content, process, and products accordingly (Tomlinson, 1999). There are many strategies that teachers can use and various ways to implement differentiated instruction. Rock, Gregg, Ellis, and Gable (2008) documented that "teachers can exercise a tremendous amount of creativity and flexibility in differentiating instruction" (p. 34). This chapter will describe tiered instruction and provide an example of a tiered lesson that was implemented by co-teachers in a fifth-grade classroom.

The Strategy of Tiered Instruction

Tiered instruction is a major teaching strategy that can be easily applied when general and special education teachers collaborate and include students with autism spectrum disorders (ASD) in the general education classroom. Richards and Omdal (2007) investigated the effects of tiered instruction on the academic performance of students in general education secondary science classes. The results from their study indicated that tiered instruction was "an effective way to increase academic achievement for lower achieving students" (Richards & Omdal, 2007, p. 447). Teachers can tier many components of the curriculum such as assessments, lessons, assignments, homework, activities for practice, materials, presentations, learning centers, and writing prompts. Tiered instruction allows all students to access the content, activities, and/or product at each student's particular level based on their characteristics of readiness, interests, and/or learning preferences (profile). Teachers can develop any number of tiers when using a particular method for instruction (e.g., activity, homework, learning center). A tiered lesson is often used to address student readiness (i.e., student ability and background knowledge) and typically has three tiers: above grade level, at grade level, and below grade level. The grouping of students for each tier should vary, however; it should be flexible so that students are not labeled by a particular "ability" or tiered group. Teachers can readily assign students to a variety of groups and tasks throughout the day and week by varying the materials to be presented, the assignments to be completed, the number of tiers for instruction, and by using students' interests and learning preferences. It is important to ensure that students with disabilities, and particularly students with ASD, are supported within their assigned tiered group. This assistance can vary depending on the student's level of comfort within a group. For example, some students may be more apt to learn a concept or skill if they are paired with a familiar partner rather than with a larger group of peers.

Planning for Tiered Instruction With an Example

There are a number of strategies that will help in organizing and planning for differentiated and tiered instruction (e.g., Chapman & King, 2008; Gregory & Chapman, 2007; Rock et al., 2008; Tomlinson, 2001; Tomlinson & Edison, 2003a, 2003b). When applying tiered instruction initially, tier only one part of the lesson or unit (*content, process,* or *product;* Pierce & Adams, 2004, p. 60). The steps shown in Table 10-1 are a guide and can be modified to meet individual classroom needs. As you use tiered instruction and become more comfortable with it, you can tier additional components within any one lesson. Also shown in Table 10-1 is a lesson that was developed by fifth-grade general and special education co-teachers. The 24 fifth graders in their class were diverse in cultures, socioeconomic status, and ability; five of the students had individualized education programs (IEPs).

Table 10-1	
Tiered Lesson in Geometry on Three Angles	
Steps for Planning Tiered Instruction	**Example of a Fifth Grade Tiered Lesson**
1. Identify a particular content standard and the key concept or skill for learning.	1. For their elementary mathematics unit the teachers centered class instruction on their state's standard of understanding basic geometric concepts. Based on their state's learning expectation of "the student will classify angles as right, acute or obtuse," the teachers differentiated their lessons using Tomlinson and Eidson (2003; pp. 95-127) as a resource guide.
2. Assess the prior knowledge or prerequisite skills needed for your students to learn the new concept or skill.	2. After a full week of lessons on angles, the teachers felt that the students had learned the concepts and skills being taught related to the three angles.
3. Decide the element of differentiated instruction (content, process, or product) that you want to tier. Base this decision on whether you want the students to be presented with different content or ways to access the content, different methods or activities for students to help them understand the concept or practice the skill, or different products that show that the students comprehend the new concept or learned the new skill.	3. They decided to assess students' understanding of right, acute, and obtuse angles by adapting the product (a culminating assessment task).
4. Determine if the element of differentiated instruction that you selected (content, process, or product) will be tiered by addressing one of the student characteristics of readiness, interests, or learning preferences.	4. To do so, they used their students' background knowledge (readiness) to tier the lesson's assignment. The co-teachers also incorporated some choices within each readiness tier based on student preferences.

Table 10-1 *(continued)*

Tiered Lesson in Geometry on Three Angles	
Steps for Planning Tiered Instruction	**Example of a Fifth Grade Tiered Lesson**
5. Develop a preassessment related to the new concept or skill based on which student characteristic (student readiness, interests or learning preferences) you selected to tier. If student characteristic data on interests and learning preferences are already available then use this infor-mation if it applies to learning the new concept or skill. If not, use an informal inventory to assess your student interests or learning preferences. If using readiness, identify your students' background knowledge by using a pretest.	5. To start, the teachers used their observational checklists of student performance and the students' work portfolios to ensure that students were ready for this assessment and to guide them later on in selecting students for each of their three readiness tiers.
6. Develop the lesson as you generally would at grade level including how you are going to assess student learning (i.e., formative and/or summative assessment) of the new concept or skill. For the instructional component of this lesson that you plan to tier, identify the number of tiers you need based on which element of differ-entiated instruction (content, process, or product) and which student characteristic (student readiness, interests or learning preferences) you selected.	6. The teachers adapted the product (the culminating assessment task of identifying the three angles) based on student readiness. The teachers used three tiers: Tier 1 (learners below grade level), Tier 2 (learners at grade level), and Tier 3 (learners above grade level). The teachers also incorporated student interests. They had students use magazines and/or draw pictures to show their understanding of the three different angles.

Table 10-1 *(continued)*

Tiered Lesson in Geometry on Three Angles	
Steps for Planning Tiered Instruction	**Example of a Fifth Grade Tiered Lesson**
7. Adjust the element of differentiated instruction (content, process, or product) that you chose by the number of tiers you selected to adapt that element based on one of the student characteristics (student readiness, interests or learning preferences). Start with that element from your lesson and then modify it incorporating the number of levels needed. For example, if you are addressing readiness, then start with the general level you used when developing your lesson and adapt that component by level of difficulty or complexity (e.g., create two new tiers of that lesson plan element to accommodate students who are below grade level and above grade level). If using interests or learning profile, "you may control the number of tiers by limiting choices or using only a few learning styles" (Pierce & Adams, 2004, p. 63).	7a. The teachers developed the assignment for the three tiers starting with the middle tier (Tier 2). This tier consisted of students who were assessed as being at approximately grade level for the lessons completed prior to this assessment. The students were given a Frayer model template (graphic organizer) for each of the three angles. In the middle of each template, they were requested to write the name of one of the angles studied and then draw a representation of that angle. Then they were asked to complete the graphic organizer which included the angle's definition and characteristics as well as providing additional examples and non examples of the angle. For the examples and non-examples, they were requested to use the internet, magazines, newspapers, or their own drawings to provide pictorial representations of each angle. The students were provided with a protractor with the marking at 90 degrees to assist them in checking the correctness of their angles.
	7b. For Tier 1 (learners below grade level), the teachers adapted the product (assignment) by providing the students with a graphic organizer which was divided in four sections; three of the sections named each angle and the fourth section was labeled as nonangles. The students were also given different colored shapes that were strategically outlined to highlight one of the three angles or a curved area. They were requested to classify the highlighted part of each shape and glue it under the correct label on their graphic organizer. Once they finished classifying their shapes, they were asked to find one picture in a magazine, newspaper or on the internet or to draw one depicting each of the angles studied and glue them with their shapes under the correct label on their angle template. The students were given a square to use for measuring their angles and nonangles.

Table 10-1 *(continued)*	
Tiered Lesson in Geometry on Three Angles	
	7c. For Tier 3 (learners above grade level), the teachers adapted the product (assignment) by giving the students an angle graphic organizer. On this organizer they were required to draw the three angles and use the geometric characteristics of each angle to compare and contrast them. When the students finished this part of the assignment, they were requested to find two objects in their environment that used more than one of these angles and one object that used no angles. Then they were asked to draw each object and explain why the angles, and the nonangle, supported the structure of the object it represented. The students were provided with a protractor with the markings at 0, 30, 60, 90, 120, 150 and 180 degrees to assist them in checking the correctness of their angles.
8. Match your students to the appropriate tier and then make adjustments to meet additional needs of individual students (e.g., scaffolding, peer assistance).	8. The co-teachers assigned students based on their observational checklist and the students' work portfolios completed that week. Tier 1 was adapted for one student who was provided with templates of a right, obtuse, and acute angle to help him measure and classify the angles. The name of each angle was printed on its corresponding template and on his graphic organizer. Peer assistance was also provided as needed.

Note. *Steps for Planning Tiered Instruction* are adapted from text within "Tiered Lessons: One Way to Differentiate Mathematics Instruction," by R. L. Pierce and C. M. Adams, 2004, *Gifted Child Today, 27*, pp. 58-64. Copyright 2004 by Sage Publications Inc. Journals.

Summary

Teachers can address students' readiness level, interests, and learning preferences across content, process, and/or product within an individual component of instruction, a lesson, or a unit. Teacher collaboration and differentiated instruction are processes that take time to develop. By working incrementally, practicing, and focusing on the objectives of students with ASD, teachers can effectively and successfully include students with ASD with their peers in general education instruction (Kilham, 2009).

References

Chapman, C., & King, R. (2008). *Differentiated instructional management: Work smarter, not harder.* Thousand Oaks, CA: Corwin Press.

Gregory, G. H., & Chapman, C. (2007). *Differentiated instructional strategies: One size doesn't fit all* (2nd ed.). Thousand Oaks, CA: Corwin Press.

Kilham, C. H. (2009). Online wiki collaboration by teachers of students with autism spectrum disorders. *Australasian Journal of Special Education, 33,* 117-129.

Pierce, R. L., & Adams, C. M. (2004). Tiered lessons: One way to differentiate mathematics instruction. *Gifted Child Today, 27,* 58-64.

Richards, M. R. E., & Omdal S. N. (2007). Effects of tiered instruction on academic performance in a secondary science course. *Journal of Advanced Academics, 18,* 424-453.

Rock, M. L., Gregg, M., Ellis, E., & Gable, R. A. (2008). REACH: A framework for differentiating instruction. *Preventing School Failure, 52,* 31-47.

Tomlinson, C. A. (1999). *The differentiated classroom: Responding to the needs of all learners.* Alexandria, VA: Association for Supervision and Curriculum Development.

Tomlinson, C. A. (2001). *How to differentiate instruction in mixed-ability classrooms* (2nd ed.). Alexandria, VA: Association for Supervision and Curriculum Development.

Tomlinson, C. A., & Eidson, C. C. (2003a). *Differentiation in practice: A resource guide for differentiating curriculum: Grades K-5.* Alexandria, VA: Association for Supervision and Curriculum Development.

Tomlinson, C. A., & Eidson, C. C. (2003b). *Differentiation in practice: A resource guide for differentiating curriculum: Grades 5-9.* Alexandria, VA: Association for Supervision and Curriculum Development.

Additional Resources

Anderson, K. A. (2007). Tips for teaching: Differentiating instruction to include all students. *Preventing School Failure, 51*, 49-54.

Lewis, S. G., & Batts, K. (2005). How to implement differentiated instruction. *National Staff Development Council, 26*, 26-31.

Perner, D. (2004). *Changing teaching practices, using curriculum differentiation to respond to students' diversity.* Paris, France: United Nations Educational, Scientific, and Cultural Organization. Retrieved from http://unesdoc.unesco.org/images/0013/001365/136583e.pdf

Tomlinson, C. A., & McTighe, J. (2006). *Integrating differentiated instruction and understanding by design.* Alexandria, VA: Association for Supervision and Curriculum Development.

van Garderen, D., & Whittaker, C. (2006). Planning differentiated, multicultural instruction for secondary inclusive classrooms. *Exceptional Children, 38*, 12-20.

Wormeli, R. (2007). *Differentiation: From planning to practice; Grades 6-12.* Portland, ME: Stenhouse.

Internet Resources

http://aim.cast.org/learn/historyarchive/backgroundpapers
This is a National Center on Accessible Instructional Materials (AIM) web page that provides background papers from the National Center on Accessing the General Curriculum (NCAC) Publications. Relevant papers include Differentiated Instruction, Implications for UDL Implementation, Graphic Organizers, Graphic Organizers with UDL, and Background Knowledge with UDL.

Internet4Classrooms at http://www.internet4classrooms.com/di.htm
This web site provides links to articles and other resources on differentiated instruction under the major topics of classroom planning, instructional theory, learning styles, meta-links sites, sample plans/lessons, helpful documents, and grading projects.

http://www.ocali.org/up_archive_doc/DI_Internet_Resources.pdf
This web site provides links to many free resources for differentiating content such as sites that include reading material at different levels, classic audio books and digital text resources.

http://unesdoc.unesco.org/images/0013/001365/136583e.pdf
This is a book published by the United Nations Educational, Scientific, and Cultural Organization and is also presented in pdf format. It includes five modules for curriculum differentiation which focus on student characteristics, and strategies related to a positive classroom environment, assessment and instruction.

Developing Reading Skills[1]

Monica E. Delano and Kelly Whalon

Challenges with language and communication development are characteristic of children with autism spectrum disorders (ASD). Most children with ASD start to speak later and develop language at a much slower rate than typically developing peers (Tager-Flusberg, Paul, & Lord, 2005). Difficulties with expressive and receptive language persist in school-age children with autism and may be a significant obstacle to the development of literacy skills. Federal education law mandates that students with ASD receive access to the general education curriculum, and that reading instruction include evidence-based instructional methods such as those advocated by the National Reading Panel (NRP; National Institute of Child Health and Human Development, 2000). Yet, there is a limited body of research to guide teachers in providing reading instruction to students with ASD (Whalon, Al Otaiba, & Delano, 2009). Given this lack of evidence-based practices, teachers may consider a few options. First, they can work with the child's family to identify meaningful literacy goals based upon the family's preferences and priorities. Next, teachers may examine evidence-based practices for teaching literacy skills to other populations of students and use or adapt these methods for learners with ASD. Collaborating with general education teachers and reading specialists to provide access to the general education curriculum will be critical. Another approach is to apply practices that are effective in teaching other skills to students with ASD (e.g., systematic instruction) to teaching literacy. Finally, teachers may consult the available literature on teaching literacy skills to students with ASD. It is likely that educators will need to use a combination all of these options to develop effective literacy instruction for learners with ASD.

[1]The authors wish to acknowledge the support of the Nystrand-Offutt Scholar Program and the Nystrand Center of Educational Excellence.

A thorough discussion of literacy instruction is beyond the scope of this chapter. Rather the purpose of this chapter is to provide educators with information about several specific strategies they may incorporate into a comprehensive classroom reading program. Methods for teaching written expression skills are addressed in Chapter 12. The strategies discussed in this chapter are based upon evidence-based practices for students with ASD or evidence-based practices for teaching reading to other student populations.

Shared Reading: A Good Place to Start and an Important Activity to Continue

One of the best things caregivers and teachers can do to support the language and literacy development of young children is to read to them frequently. Shared reading provides a rich context for adults and children to engage in meaningful interaction. When specific shared reading approaches (e.g., dialogic reading) are implemented children with language delays speak more, increase their mean length of utterance, and increase their vocabulary diversity (Crain-Thoreson & Dale, 1999). Research also suggests that shared reading has a positive impact on the emergent literacy skills of preschool children (Whitehurst et al., 1994; Whitehurst et al., 1999) and may be a more effective language facilitation intervention than play-based strategies for children with language delays (Dale, Crain-Thoreson, Norari-Syverson, & Cole, 1996).

Though the benefits of shared reading have been well-documented in children with language delays, research is just emerging on the use of shared reading with children who have more complex support needs, such as ASD. In addition to supporting the development of emergent literacy skills, shared reading may be well suited to address the language and communication challenges faced by children with ASD. Like other naturalistic interventions (see Chapter 6) for teaching communication, shared reading provides a means for communication partners to model, expand, and support social communication. It also engages children in joint attention, an important instructional target for children on the autism spectrum in developing communication skills. Thus, incorporating shared reading into literacy instruction has many potential benefits to both younger and older students on the autism spectrum. This section of the chapter will discuss preparation for shared reading lessons and describe two approaches to shared reading that may be effective with students with ASD: dialogic reading and the use of systematic instruction (see Chapter 4).

Prior to implementing shared reading, teachers must identify instructional targets for children with ASD. Shared reading is a useful context in which to address instructional goals related to vocabulary, language development, communication, emergent literacy, comprehension, and narrative structure. After teachers identify instructional targets, they must develop a progress monitoring system to track children's development over time. In addition, teachers must determine the communicative form students will use to respond during shared reading and identify any necessary supports (e.g., AAC devices).

Selecting Books for Shared Reading

There are several factors to consider when selecting books for shared reading. First, it is important that books are age appropriate. For young children this task will be relatively simple. Books with colorful illustrations, predictable text, repeated story lines, or rhyme may be particularly engaging. Though some books may need to be adapted for younger children, adaptations will more likely be necessary to provide older students with access to age appropriate literature. Adaptations will vary based upon the student's skills, but may include elements such as shortened and simplified text (e.g., shortening a full-length novel to a brief summary), adding objects or pictures to support communication and comprehension, and adding a repeated story line. Several studies of shared reading with students with autism or moderate to severe disabilities (e.g., Browder, Trela, & Jimenez, 2007; Mims, Browder, Baker, Lee, & Spooner, 2009) have incorporated these adaptations and serve as good models for teachers. Lewis and Tolla (2003) also provide a wealth of suggestions for adapting books (see the resource list at the end of the chapter).

Second, it is critical for teachers to select books that are written on an appropriate language level for the child. Shared reading is an excellent method to teach new vocabulary, but listening comprehension will be negatively impacted if too much of the vocabulary is new to the student. Providing students with choices, making certain books match the children's interest and identifying books that have connections to children's experiences are important considerations. Based upon the children's characteristics, it is also useful to consider the length of the reading session and select books that are appropriate for the time selected.

Adapted Dialogic Reading for Children With ASD

Dialogic reading is one form of shared reading. It uses a specific set of prompts to target children's oral language and listening comprehension (Justice & Pullen, 2003) and to improve the quality of adult-child interactions. In other words, by using dialogic reading strategies adults can be responsive communication partners and can facilitate children's language development. Children and teachers engage in multiple readings of storybooks. During initial readings the teacher focuses on building vocabulary, however during additional readings the focus will be on expanding language, encouraging the child to talk more, and supporting comprehension of the story (Zevenbergen & Whitehurst, 2003). The authors of this chapter developed an adapted version of dialogic reading to support beginning communicators with disabilities such as autism spectrum disorders. Their adaptation of dialogic reading is called *Reading to Engage Children with Autism in Language and Learning* or RECALL (Whalon, Delano, & Hanline, in press).

Two acronyms assist adults in implementing traditional dialogic strategies: PEER and CROWD. PEER, provides teachers with a structure for scaffolding interactions with children during shared reading activities (**P**—prompt or pose a question, **E**—evaluate the child's response, **E**—expand on the child's response, **R**—have the child repeat the expansion; Zevenbergen & Whitehurst, 2003). To support beginning communicators on the autism spectrum RECALL modifies the PEER sequence by including a prompt hierarchy as illustrated in Table 11-1. The prompt hierarchy provides a means for teachers to explicitly teach children to respond to questions. Each time the child answers a question, the teacher has an opportunity to expand the child's language. Use of the PEER sequence engages the child, builds vocabulary, and gradually expands the child's language. However, in order to facilitate growth in language and communication, it is critical that adults are responsive to all communicative attempts and provide children on the autism spectrum with many opportunities to initiate. Because children with ASD often display a low rate of initiations, it may be useful to incorporate elements of naturalistic language interventions into shared reading. Examples of useful strategies include (a) maintaining a balance of adult-child turns, (b) talking at the child's level, (c) following the child's interest, (d) moving on if the child loses interest (e.g., turn page, change books, or end reading session), (e) pausing expectantly to provide opportunities for the child to initiate, and (f) creating "silly situations" (Kaiser, Hancock, & Nietfeld, 2000). During reading sessions, teachers need not focus on reading every word of the book. Instead teachers use the book as a context for communicating with the child and use responsive communication strategies to support the child's language and participation in the interaction.

The second acronym used in traditional dialogic reading, CROWD, suggests types of questions that the teacher may pose during shared reading. These questions include **C**ompletion prompts in which the child is asked to provide that last word in a line (this may be a repeated story line or rhyme), **R**ecall questions, **O**pen-ended questions, "**W**h-questions," and **D**istancing questions which ask questions that let the child make connections between the story and real life (see Zevenbergen & Whitehurst, 2003 for a description of PEER and CROWD). In order to support children with autism, RECALL adds several prompts to the CROWD sequence (see Table 11-2). It is important to remember that some children on the autism spectrum have difficulty developing question-answering skills (Jahr, 2001). Therefore, it may be useful to introduce types of questions gradually, instead of using the whole CROWD sequence initially. In addition to asking questions, it is important to pause and provide opportunities for the child to initiate. Visual cues may be used to support the child in asking specific questions. The types of questions targeted (for both initiating and responding) will depend upon the child's language and communication skills.

Table 11-1

The PEER Sequence and a Systematic Prompt Hierarchy	
Dialogic Reading PEER Sequence[a]	**Prompt Hierarchy RECALL**[b]

Prompt the child to say something about the book.
 	
Evaluate the child's response.
 	
Expand the child's response by adding more information.
 	
Repeat the expansion.
	Prompting Hierarchy
	1. Follow the PEER sequence by asking the child to say something about the book (e.g., *"What is the girl doing in the picture?"*).
	2. If the child responds correctly, provide praise and continue the PEER sequence
	3. If the child does not respond in 3-5 seconds or responds incorrectly, the teacher provides a binary choice (e.g., *"Is the girl jumping or eating?"*).
	  • If the child responds correctly, praise and expand on the child's response (e.g., *"Yes, the girl is jumping on her bed."*).
	  • If the child does not respond or responds incorrectly, deliver the next prompt in the hierarchy.
	4. Model a response (e.g., *"The girl is jumping."*)
	  • If the child imitates the model, provide praise and expand on the child's response (e.g., *"Yes, the girl is jumping on her bed."*).
	  • If the child does not imitate the model, restate the question and repeat the model prompt. If the child imitates the model, provide praise and expand the child's response.
	  • If the child does not respond correctly and is still attending, provide the direct model again (e.g., *"The girl is jumping."*) and ask the child to repeat the model.
	  • If the child does not imitate the model and is no longer attending, regain the child's attention (e.g., verbally prompt the child to look at a picture in the book) and begin reading again. When the child is attending, pause and begin the PEER sequence again by asking the child to say something about the book (e.g., *"Where is the girl going?"*).

Note. [a] Zevenbergen, A., & Whitehurst, G. J. (2003). Dialogic reading: A shared picture book reading intervention for preschoolers. In A. van Kleeck, S. Stahl, & E. Bauer (Eds.), *On reading books to children* (pp. 177-200). Mahwah, NJ: Lawrence Erlbaum Associates. [b] Whalon, K., & Hanline, M. F. (2008). Effects of reciprocal questioning on the question generation and responding of children with autism spectrum disorders. *Education and Training in Developmental Disabilities, 43,* 367-387.

Table 11-2

Dialogic Reading CROWD Sequence[a]
Completion: A blank is left at the end of a sentence and the child fills it in (e.g., "*There were clothes everywhere*.").
Recall: Questions about what has already happened in the book (e.g., "*Where did Tia find her glove?*").
Open-Ended: Questions with open-ended responses (e.g., Ask the child to tell what is happening in the picture).
Wh-questions: who, what where, when, why, and how.
Distancing: Questions that help children relate information from the book to their own experiences (e.g., "*Have you ever broken something like Alexander?*").
RECALL Program Prompts[b]
Emotion identification: Questions about how the characters may be feeling about events in the story (e.g., "*How do you think Wilbur feels?*").
Secure attention: A statement and/or gesture attempting to elicit joint attention (e.g., "*Look!*" while pointing to a picture).
Initiation: Scripted question cards or visual supports are available at three points during the reading.
Intentional pause: At three different points in the story before or after turning a page, the teacher will pause for 5-seconds while looking expectantly at the child to encourage initiation.

Note. [a] Zevenbergen, A., & Whitehurst, G. J. (2003). Dialogic reading: A shared picture book reading intervention for preschoolers. In A. van Kleeck, S. Stahl, & E. Bauer (Eds.), *On reading books to children* (pp. 177-200). Mahwah, NJ: Lawrence Erlbaum Associates. [b] Whalon, K., & Hanline, M. F. (2008). Effects of reciprocal questioning on the question generation and responding of children with autism spectrum disorders. *Education and Training in Developmental Disabilities, 43,* 367-387.

The CROWD sequence provides a useful framework. Teachers who read dialogically to children on the autism spectrum provide children with many opportunities to respond during storybook reading and support children's language development and listening comprehension in a meaningful context.

Applying Systematic Instruction During Shared Reading

Browder and her colleagues (e.g., Browder et al., 2007; Mims et al., 2009) have applied systematic instructional strategies such as task analysis and system of least prompts to shared reading activities. This work suggests the benefits of teachers using familiar instructional procedures to improve engagement, emergent literacy, and comprehension skills. Teachers follow a task analysis that identifies the steps they will complete during a shared reading lesson (e.g., asking a prediction question, giving students opportunities to anticipate a repeated storyline, asking comprehension questions). Teachers also develop a prompt hierarchy and use a task analysis to identify the steps the student will complete during shared reading sessions (e.g., repeating vocabulary word, answering comprehension question, pointing to text). During shared reading the teachers implement a least-to-most prompt system to support the student's participation in the reading activity. Teachers should consult Browder & Spooner (2011) for additional information about this promising approach (see the resource list at the end of the chapter).

Reading books to children is an important way to develop communication and literacy skills and there are opportunities to engage in shared reading in typical educational environments. Though research on the use of shared reading with students on the autism spectrum is just emerging, it seems likely that students with ASD may benefit from this instructional activity.

Supporting Comprehension Through Reciprocal Teaching

Many children with ASD will learn to effectively decode words in text, but will struggle with reading comprehension (Calhoon, 2001; Leekam, 2007; Lord & Paul, 1997; Mayes & Calhoun 2003a, 2003b; Nation, Clarke, Wright, & Williams, 2006; Wahlberg & Magliano, 2004). The NRP (National Institute of Child Health and Human Development, 2000) recommends explicit reading comprehension strategy instruction to address reading comprehension (NCLB 2001; IDEA 2004). Reading comprehension failure is generally linked to an inability to make inferences, gauge understanding, and/or predict narrative structure (Oakhill & Cain, 2007). Explicit comprehension instruction, as suggested by the NRP, addresses these skills by directly teaching the cognitive processes necessary to comprehend text (Perfetti, Landi, & Oakhill, 2005).

Intervention studies that incorporated methods consistent with NRP recommendations to address the reading comprehension of students with ASD reported gains on vocabulary and/or comprehension quizzes (Dugan et al., 1995; Kamps, Barbetta, Leonard, & Delquadri, 1994; Kamps, Leonard, Potucek, & Garrison-Harrell, 1995; Kamps, Locke, Delquadri, & Hall, 1989), generating and responding to questions during reading (Whalon & Hanline, 2008), identifying causes of events in a scenario (Flores & Ganz, 2007), and retelling important story details (O'Connor & Klein, 2004). Although preliminary, this emerging evidence base suggests that children with ASD can (a) benefit from comprehension instruction consistent with NRP recommendations (Chiang & Lin, 2007; Whalon et al., 2009), and (b) learn to apply the cognitive processes necessary for generating meaning (Randi, Newman, & Grigorenko, 2010).

Multi-Method Comprehension Instruction

The NRP found that question generation was the single most effective reading comprehension strategy (National Institute of Child Health and Human Development [NICHD], 2000); however, research indicates that effective readers use a number of strategies during reading to support comprehension (Pressley, 2003). Consequently, the NRP concluded that children should be taught multiple comprehension strategies to include two or more of the following: question generation, summarization, clarification, and prediction (NICHD, 2000).

Reciprocal teaching (RT) is a multi-method reading comprehension strategy developed specifically for readers who effectively decode text, but experience difficulty comprehending it. Reciprocal teaching is often used with individuals who score below the 35th percentile on standardized reading comprehension measures (Palinscar & Herrenkohl, 2002). In RT, roles are reciprocal as teachers and students take turns facilitating discussions about a text (Palinscar & Herrenkohl, 2002). Following reciprocal teaching, learners with effective decoding and poor reading comprehension skills (Lysynchuk, Pressley, & Vye, 1990; Palinscar & Brown, 1984), and students with mild disabilities (Marston, Deno, Dongil, Diment, & Rogers, 1995) have improved their reading comprehension. Reciprocal teaching not only leads to increased performance on comprehension assessments, but also improves the quality of discussions about text (Lipson & Wixson, 2009). With deliberate scaffolding, reciprocal teaching was used with students as young as first grade to teach early science content (Palinscsar & Brown, 1986).

RT discussions are comprised of four components, (1) predicting, (2) question generation, (3) clarifying, and (4) summarizing. Before reading, the teacher designates a number of stopping points throughout the text for students to apply each RT component. When the group reaches each predetermined stopping point, the facilitator generates questions that focus on the main ideas presented in the text. Students respond to posed questions and ask additional questions. When unsure of the answer, the group refers back to the reading and the facilitator or teacher helps them locate the correct response. Following questioning, students summarize the author's message, and clarify the meaning of words, concepts, and/or phrases that may impact understanding. Prior to reading the next predetermined section of text, students predict. Prediction requires students to infer what will happen in the text (Palinscar & Herrenkohl, 2002).

The teacher initially facilitates RT, using "think aloud" by walking students through the mental processes used to apply each strategy. Students practice the strategies as the teacher monitors and provides feedback (Pressley, 2000). As students are able to independently apply RT, the teacher's role changes to coach (Palinscar & Herrenkohl, 2002). At that point, the students take turns as leaders while reading different portions of the text as the teacher provides feedback. The goal is to fade instruction as the students become responsible for self-monitoring their use of RT (Wilkinson & Silliman, 2000). Table 11-3 is an example of dialogue that could be used to introduce the RT strategies with students in first grade using the book *Born to Be a Butterfly* by Karen Wallace.

When working with learners with ASD, teachers may need to adapt RT. In their review of the RT literature, Rosenshine and Meister (1994) found that when initially teaching the RT strategies, some researchers used smaller portions of text. For example, when teaching question generation, some authors taught students to generate questions from sentences prior to applying the strategy when reading text. In addition, to facilitate learning and application of the strategies, many researchers incorporated procedural prompts. That is, many studies included question words such as who, what, when, where, why, and how or generic questions to help students generate questions about text. Other studies provided steps for summarizing portions of text that included identifying the main details, and using these details to create a summary (Rosenshine & Meister, 1994). Figure 11-1 includes sample cue cards for each of the reciprocal teaching strategies. Similar prompting techniques are found in the ASD literature. For example, visual cues, scripted comments/questions, and self-monitoring checklists have been used to teach children with ASD a variety of skills (See Earles-Vollrath, Cook, Robbins, & Ben-Arieh, 2008).

Conclusion

Changes in federal laws over the past decade have raised academic expectations, and (for the first time in history) required that all students have access to and make progress in the general education curriculum. Thus, students with ASD will have an opportunity to learn academic skills and participate in a rich curriculum. Unfortunately, research has not yet provided a clear path for teaching reading and other academic skills to students with more complex support needs. This chapter provides educators with information about several specific strategies that may be incorporated into a comprehensive classroom literacy program. These strategies may be implemented in inclusive settings and are based upon evidence-based practices for students with ASD or evidence-based practices for teaching reading to other populations of students.

Table 11-3

Sample Scaffolding of Reciprocal Teaching Steps		
RT Component	**Introducing Component**	**Applying Component**
Predicting	"If I told you that I am going to predict what game you are going to play at recess, what do I mean by predict?" "That's right, I am going to make a guess. I would guess that many of you will play kickball because you had such a good time playing kickball yesterday. So, when I predict, I use what I already know to help me make a guess."	"The story we are reading is called, *Born to Be a Butterfly*. What is a butterfly?" "Yes, it is an insect. What does it do?" "Right, butterflies fly and get their food from flowers. Do you think this story is fiction or nonfiction?" "Good, nonfiction. How can you tell?" "That's true, the picture of the butterfly is a real butterfly and not a cartoon." "Yes, we have read other books like this one that were nonfiction. Nice job using what you know to help you predict. Okay, what do you think the story will be about – *Born to Be a Butterfly?*"
Questioning	"Good readers ask questions when they read. Asking questions helps us remember what is important in the story. Good questions start with a question word. We have our question cue cards to remind us of our question words [points to the cue cards while reading] who, what, when, where, why, and how."	*Text: "The caterpillar is hungry. She needs to grow so she crawls from her leaf tent. She climbs up strong stems and clings to young leaves. The caterpillar munches and crunches all the leaves she can find."* Teacher: "We need to ask a question about what we just read. What is something that we just learned here?" Student 1: "Caterpillars are hungry and eat a lot." Teacher: "That's right. We also learned what a caterpillar eats. Will you ask a question about that? Remember to use a question word." Student 1: "What does the caterpillar munch and crunch?" Teacher: "Great question!" Student 2: "All the leaves she can find." Teacher: "Excellent! You found that answer right in your book. She eats all the leaves she can find, and if caterpillars live in trees, I bet they find a lot of leaves. Caterpillars must be really hungry! I wonder why they eat so much. I have a question, [picks up the why question cue card] Why do you think caterpillars eat so much?"

Table 11-3 *(continued)*

Sample Scaffolding of Reciprocal Teaching Steps		
RT Component	**Introducing Component**	**Applying Component**
Clarifying	"Sometimes when we read we come to a big word that we don't know. If we don't know a word, we need to clarify what it means. That means we have to be detectives and figure out what that word means. How can we figure out what a word means? We can ask someone, or we can look it up in our dictionary."	Now I know we talked about this word when we talked about flowers, but I'm having trouble remembering what it means. Would someone tell me, what is nectar?" Student: "It's like a sugar juice that comes from plants." Teacher: "That's right. Remember that when we come to a word we don't know, we clarify."
Summarizing	"When we finish reading a section, we want to summarize what we read. Summarize means to tell about the story in a few words. So, do we try to remember every word? No. We want to tell about the story using only a few words, so we have to remember all of the important ideas."	*Text: "The caterpillar grows quickly. She sheds her skin four times before she is fully grown. She looks for a leaf that is sturdy and strong. She hangs upside down. The caterpillar is changing into a chrysalis. Outside, her skin turns hard to keep her safe. Inside, something amazing is happening."* "Before we go on to the next section we have to summarize. Remember that when we summarize we only tell about the important details. What is the most important thing we learned? Student 1: "The caterpillar is growing." "Okay, good, the caterpillar is growing. What else is happening to the caterpillar?" Student 2: "The caterpillars skin is changing into a chrysalis." "Great. So the caterpillar is growing up and turning into a chrysalis."

Note. RT = Reciprocal Teaching.

Figure 11-1

Cue Cards for Reciprocal Teaching

Predict.

What do you think will happen next?

Clarify.

1. Find the trouble words.
2. Ask someone for clarification.

Ask a Question.

Pick a Question Word:
Who, What, When, Where, Why, How

Example:
Who or what is this section about?
What happened to _____?
What does _____ do?
Why did _____ do that?

Summarize.

1. Who or what is this section about?
2. Number the main details.
3. Put the main details in order.
4. Make a statement using each detail.
5. Make sure your statement has less than 12 words.
6. Say your statement.

References

Browder, D. M., & Spooner, F. (2011). *Teaching students with moderate and severe disabilities.* New York, NY: Guilford Press.

Browder, D. M., Trela, K., & Jimenez, B. (2007). Training teachers to follow a task analysis to engage middle school students with moderate and severe disabilities in grade-appropriate literature. *Focus on Autism and Other Developmental Disabilities, 22,* 206-219.

Calhoon, J. A. (2001). Factors affecting the reading of rimes in words and nonwords in beginning readers with cognitive disabilities and typically developing readers. *Journal of Autism and Developmental Disorders, 31,* 491-504.

Chiang, H., & Lin, Y. (2007). Reading comprehension instruction for students with autism spectrum disorders: A review of the literature. *Focus on Autism and Other Developmental Disabilities, 22,* 259-267.

Crain-Thoreson, C., & Dale, P. (1999). Enhancing linguistic performance: Parents and teachers as book reading partners for children with language delays. *Topics in Early Childhood Special Education, 19,* 28-39.

Dale, P. S., Crain-Thoreson, C., Norari-Syverson, A., & Cole, K. (1996). Parent-child book reading as an intervention for young children with language delays. *Topics in Early Childhood Special Education, 16,* 213-235.

Dugan, E., Kamps, D., Leonard, B., Watkins, N., Rheinberger, A., & Stackhaus, J. (1995). Effects of cooperative learning groups during social studies for students with autism and fourth-grade peers. *Journal of Applied Behavior Analysis, 28,* 175-188.

Earles-Vollrath, T. L., Cook, K. T., Robbins, L., & Ben-Arieh, J. (2008). Instructional strategies to facilitate successful learning outcomes for students with autism spectrum disorders. In R. L. Simpson & B. S. Myles (Eds.), *Educating children and youth with autism: Strategies for effective practice* (2nd ed., pp. 222-243). Austin, TX: Pro-Ed.

Flores, M., & Ganz, J. (2007). Effectiveness of direct instruction for teaching statement inference, use of facts, and analogies to students with developmental disabilities and reading delays. *Focus on Autism and Other Developmental Disabilities, 22,* 244–251.

Individuals With Disabilities Education Improvement Act, 20 U.S.C. § 1400 *et seq.* (2004).

Jahr, E. (2001). Teaching children with autism to answer novel wh-questions by utilizing a multiple exemplar strategy. *Research in Developmental Disabilities, 22,* 407-423.

Justice, L. M., & Pullen, P. C. (2003). Promising interventions for promoting emergent literacy skills: Three evidence-based approaches. *Topics in Early Childhood Special Education, 23,* 99-113.

Kaiser, A. P., Hancock, T. B., & Nietfeld, J. P. (2000). The effects of parent-implemented enhanced milieu teaching on the social communication of children who have autism. *Early Education and Development, 11,* 423-446.

Kamps, D. M., Barbetta, P. M., Leonard, B. R., & Delquadri, J. C. (1994). Classwide peer tutoring: An integration strategy to improve reading skills and promote peer interactions among students with autism and general education peers. *Journal of Applied Behavior Analysis, 27,* 49-61.

Kamps, D. M., Leonard, B., Potucek, J., & Garrison-Harrell, L. G. (1995). Cooperative learning groups in reading: An integration strategy for students with autism and general classroom peers. *Behavioral Disorders, 21,* 89-109.

Kamps, D. M., Locke, P., Delquadri, J., & Hall, R.V. (1989). Increasing academic skills of students with autism using fifth grade peers as tutors. *Education and Treatment of Children, 12,* 38-51.

Leekam, S. (2007). Language comprehension difficulties in children with autism spectrum disorders. In K. Cain & J. Oakhill (Eds.), *Children's comprehension problems in oral and writ ten language: A cognitive perspective* (pp.104-127). New York, NY: Guilford Press.

Lewis, S., & Tolla, J. (2003). Creating and using tactile experience books for young children with visual impairments. *TEACHING Exceptional Children, 35*(3), 22-28.

Lipson, M. Y., & Wixson, K. K. (2009). *Assessment and instruction of reading and writing difficulties: An interactive approach* (4th ed.). Boston, MA: Pearson.

Lord, C., & Paul, R. (1997). Language and communication in ASD. In D. J. Cohen & F. R. Volkmar (Eds.), *Handbook of ASD and pervasive developmental disorders* (2nd ed., pp. 195-225). New York, NY: John Wiley & Sons.

Lysynchuk, L. M., Pressley, M., & Vye, N. J. (1990). Reciprocal teaching improves standardized reading-comprehension performance in poor comprehenders. *The Elementary School Journal, 90,* 469-484.

Marston, D., Deno, S. L., Dongil, K., Diment, K., & Rogers, D. (1995). Comparison of reading intervention approaches for students with mild disabilities. *Exceptional Children, 62,* 20-37.

Mayes, S. D., & Calhoun, S. L. (2003a). Ability profiles in children with autism: Influence of age and IQ. *Autism, 6*, 65-80.

Mayes, S. D., & Calhoun, S. L. (2003b). Analysis of WISC-III, Stanford-Binet: IV, and academic achievement test scores in children with autism. *Journal of Autism and Developmental Disorders, 33*, 329-341.

Mims, P. J., Browder, D. M., Baker, J. N., Lee, A., & Spooner, F. (2009). Increasing comprehension of students with significant intellectual disabilities and visual impairments during shared stories. *Education and Training in Developmental Disabilities, 44*, 409-420.

Nation, K., Clarke, P., Wright, B., & Williams, C. (2006). Patterns of reading ability in children with autism spectrum disorder. *Journal of Autism and Developmental Disorders, 36*, 911- 919.

National Institute of Child Health and Human Development. (2000). *Report of the National Reading Panel. Teaching children to read: An evidence-based assessment of the scientific research literature on reading and its implications for reading instruction* (NIH Publication No. 00-4769). Washington, DC: U.S. Government Printing Office.

No Child Left Behind Act, 20 U.S.C. 70 § 6301 *et seq.* (2001).

Oakhill, J., & Cain, K. (2007). Introduction to comprehension development. In K. Cain & J. Oakhill (Eds.), *Children's comprehension problems in oral and written language: A cognitive perspective* (pp. 3-40). New York, NY: Guilford Press.

O'Connor, I. M., & Klein, P. D. (2004). Exploration of strategies for facilitating the reading comprehension of high-functioning students with autism spectrum disorders. *Journal of Autism and Developmental Disorders, 14*, 115-127.

Palincsar, A. S., & Brown, A. L. (1984). Reciprocal teaching of comprehension-fostering and comprehension-monitoring activities. *Cognition and Instruction, 2*, 117-175.

Palincsar, A. S., & Brown, A. L. (1986). Interactive teaching to promote independent learning from text. *The Reading Teacher, 39*, 771-777.

Palincsar, A. S., & Herrenkohl, L. R. (2002). Designing collaborative contexts. *Theory into Practice, 41*, 26-32.

Perfetti, C. A., Landi, N., & Oakhill, J. (2005). The acquisition of reading comprehension skill. In M. J. Snowling & C. Hulme (Eds.), *The science of reading: A handbook* (pp. 227–247). Malden, MA: Blackwell.

Pressley, M. (2000). What should comprehension instruction be the instruction of? In M. L. Kamil, P. B. Mosenthal, P. D. Pearson, & R. Barr (Eds.), *Handbook of reading research: Volume III* (pp. 333-356). Mahwah, NJ: Lawrence Erlbaum Associates.

Pressley, M. (2003). Psychology of literacy and literacy instruction. In I. B. Weiner (Series Ed.), W. M. Reynolds & G. E. Miller (Vol. Eds.), *Handbook of psychology: Vol. 7 Educational psychology* (pp. 177-198). Hoboken, NJ: John Wiley & Sons.

Randi, J., Newman, T., & Grigorenko, E. L. (2010). Teaching children with autism to read for meaning: Challenges and possibilities. *Journal of Autism and Developmental Disabilities, 40,* 890-902.

Rosenshine, B., & Meister, C. (1994). Reciprocal teaching: A review of the research. *Review of Educational Research, 64,* 479-530.

Tager-Flusberg, H., Paul, R., & Lord, C. (2005). Language and communication in autism. In F. Volkmar, R. Paul, A. Klin, & D. Cohen (Eds.) *Handbook of autism and pervasive developmental disorders* (pp. 335-364). Hoboken, NJ: John Wiley & Sons.

Wallace, K. (2000). *Born to be a butterfly.* London, England: Dorling Kindersley.

Whalon, K., Delano, M. E., & Hanline, M. F. (in press). A rationale for adapting dialogic reading for children with autism spectrum disorders. *Preventing School Failure.*

Whalon, K., & Hanline, M. F. (2008). Effects of reciprocal questioning on the question generation and responding of children with autism spectrum disorders. *Education and Training in Developmental Disabilities, 43,* 367-387.

Whalon, K. J., Al Otaiba, S., & Delano, M. (2009). Evidence based reading instruction for individuals with autism spectrum disorders. *Focus on Autism and Developmental Disabilities, 24,* 3-16.

Whitehurst, G. J., Epstein, J., Angell, A. L., Payne, A. C., Crone, D. A., & Fischel, J. E. (1994). Outcomes of an emergent literacy intervention in Head Start. *Journal of Educational Psychology, 86,* 542-555.

Whitehurst, G. J., Zevenbergen, A., Crone, D., Schultyz, M., Velting, O., & Fischel, J. (1999). Outcomes of an emergent literacy intervention from Head Start through second grade. *Journal of Educational Psychology, 91,* 261-272.

Wilkinson, L. C., & Silliman, E. R. (2000). Classroom language and literacy learning. In M. L. Kamil, P. B. Mosenthal, P. D. Pearson, & R. Barr (Eds.), *Handbook of reading research: Volume III* (pp. 337-360). Mahwah, NJ: Lawrence Erlbaum Associates.

Zevenbergen, A., & Whitehurst, G. J. (2003). Dialogic reading: A shared picture book reading intervention for preschoolers. In A. van Kleeck, S. Stahl, & E. Bauer (Eds.), *On reading books to children* (pp. 177-200). Mahwah, NJ: Lawrence Erlbaum Associates.

Additional Resources

Browder, D. M., & Spooner, F. (2011). *Teaching students with moderate and severe disabilities.* New York, NY: Guilford Press.

Copeland, S., & Keefe, E. (2007). *Effective literacy instruction for students with moderate or severe disabilities.* Baltimore, MD: Brookes.

Kleeck, A., Stahl, S., & Bauer, E. (Eds.). (2003). *On reading books to children.* Mahwah, NJ: Lawrence Erlbaum.

Kluth, P., & Chandler-Olcott, K. (2008). *A land we can share: Teaching literacy to students with autism.* Baltimore, MD: Brookes.

Lewis, S., & Tolla, J. (2003). Creating and using tactile experience books for young children with visual impairments. *TEACHING Exceptional Children, 35*(3), 22-8.

Teaching Written Expression

Monica E. Delano and Robert C. Pennington

Written expression, required for independence across a wide range of contexts, is a valuable tool for students with autism spectrum disorders (ASD). In educational settings, most students are expected to demonstrate their knowledge through written products. Writing skills also are critical to future success in many vocational settings (National Commission on Writing, 2004). Employers increasingly assess writing competencies when hiring and determining promotion. Once on the job, individuals will be required to perform a variety of tasks that involve basic to more complex writing skills. Finally, written expression has increasingly become the preferred medium for social interaction. Individuals will perform interactions daily via e-mails, texting, or social media networks (e.g., Facebook, MySpace). Those without the skills to engage in this new electronic world will find themselves increasingly isolated.

Despite the importance of writing skills, researchers have conducted few studies involving teaching written expression to students with ASD. As with reading, available research provides little guidance to educators in planning and implementing writing instruction for students with ASD. Recommendations about writing instruction for students with ASD must be based upon writing research with other populations of students, effective instructional practices for students with autism, and practices identified by the limited research base on teaching writing to students with ASD. In addition, the planning and implementation of writing instruction involves cooperation and support from a variety of professionals (e.g., classroom teachers, special educators, instructional assistants, speech language pathologists, assistive technology consultants, occupational therapist). Because writing occurs across all curricular areas, a team approach is especially critical. Also, close collaboration between the school staff and students' families will lead to the development of meaningful goals for written expression.

After discussing some initial considerations in planning writing instruction, this chapter will introduce three approaches to teaching writing: systematic instruction, computer assisted instruction, and strategy instruction. Teachers can implement these strategies in the context of a comprehensive classroom writing program and will likely find that peers will benefit from these methods as well.

Initial Considerations

There are several issues relevant to writing instruction which teachers will consider when planning supports for a student with ASD. First, an examination of the instructional context and the student's communication skills are critical initial steps in planning writing lessons. Next, a review of samples of the student's writing will enable the teacher to set appropriate goals. Finally, identifying individualized motivational strategies and supports will be critical in ensuring the student's success. Each of these issues is described in more detail in this section of the chapter.

Context

A careful review of the instructional context will help teachers plan for how the student with ASD will access writing lessons and engage in classroom activities. Questions to consider include: What are the classroom routines and expectations related to writing activities? What are the instructional goals? How do students engage in each part of the writing process? What kinds of writing tasks do students complete? What genres of writing will the teacher assign (e.g., story writing, expository writing, persuasive essays, journal writing)? Do peers collaborate on writing tasks? Do students select topics for writing assignments? How and how often does the teacher provide feedback to students? Do peers provide feedback? How do students share their writing samples? How does the teacher evaluate the students' writing samples? What kinds of supports will be beneficial to the student with ASD?

Communication

Writing is a form of communication. Students generate text through writing or typing words on paper. Some students may use alternative strategies to communicate (e.g., selecting pictures, completing a template, using assistive technology). These students may need adjustments to their communication system (e.g., new symbols on a communication device) to engage in specific writing activities. It is critical for students to have a functional means to communicate in all contexts. It is also important for all members of the educational team, as well as peers, to understand the student's communication mode.

Goals and Data Collection

Prior to instruction, the teacher collects data on the student's present writing performance and reviews grade appropriate state standards. Data may include variables such as the number of words written, number of story or essay elements, duration of planning, or a holistic score used to assess the quality of the student's writing samples. The type of data collected depends on the student's individual instructional targets as well as the content of the state standards. Educators will collaborate with the student's family to set meaningful goals for writing instruction. Goals might focus on areas such as fluency, production, content, organization, word choice, quality, planning, and revising. Goals may also address writing skills in specific contexts (e.g., using a stamp to write name on papers in class, writing an e-mail to a friend). In addition, teachers should identify individualized education program (IEP) goals that can be addressed in the context of writing activities. For example, a student with a communication goal to increase initiations during conversations with peers could work on this goal during brainstorming sessions with peers in which students work in small groups to create a list of ideas for a story.

Motivational Strategies

Initially, writing may not be a preferred activity for some students, so it is important to use motivational strategies during instruction. Teachers may interview students and caregivers, or conduct preference assessments to determine preferred topics to use during instruction. For example, when planning for instruction, a teacher might present several pictures to a student and say, "Choose one." After repeating this process several times, the teacher uses the items most often selected as the content for writing. Teachers also should determine powerful reinforcers and deliver them frequently during instruction to ensure that writing is motivating for the learner. Although traditional instructional practices may prescribe providing feedback on a student's writing sample after it has been turned in, students with ASD will likely require feedback and reinforcement during the writing process.

Supports

When writing, many students, including students with ASD, benefit from the use of visual supports. Students may use charts to complete prewriting activities (e.g., story grammar chart). Mnemonic charts may remind students of the steps to complete a specific type of writing task. Outlines provide a detailed plan. Checklists may guide the editing and revision process. Some students with ASD will benefit from more individualized supports. For example, a beginning writer with ASD may use a story template like the one illustrated in Figure 12-1. The student selects pictures or words to complete the story. Other supports include peers, the use of a scribe for parts of the writing process, or assistive technology.

Figure 12-1

Story Template

_____ went to _____.
         Character   Place

_____ _____.
         Character   Action

_____ was _____.
         Character   Emotion

Instructional Strategies

Systematic Instruction

Systematic instruction is described in detail in Chapter 4. Applying the methods outlined in Chapter 4 to teaching specific writing skills may be effective with some students on the autism spectrum. Students with ASD may demonstrate uneven development across writing skills. For example, a student may spell very complex words during weekly spelling tests but when asked, may not be able to construct a sentence about his or her activities over the weekend. During the acquisition of new skills, teachers must ensure that students are attending and that all instructions are clear and concise. It is important to consider what environmental signal will cue a student to perform a writing response in natural contexts. For instance, teaching a student to write his or her name on a piece of paper 20 times has little functional purpose, but teaching a student to write his or her name on a variety of job applications may actually increase the student's independence in natural environments. Prompting may be needed to ensure correct responses.

Writing is challenging and involves the near simultaneous execution of several skills; therefore it is important that students are provided with opportunities for success on early writing tasks. Once the student performs responses consistently, all prompts must be systematically faded. This may include inserting a brief wait time between the task directive and the delivery of a prompt (i.e., constant time delay), decreasing the amount of assistance provided (i.e., most to least prompting) or by slowly fading the amount of information of a given model (i.e., antecedent stimulus fading). After a student demonstrates the targeted writing skill, he or she must have the opportunity to demonstrate the skill in different contexts and for less reinforcement. If the student cannot execute the new skill in different contexts, additional instruction will be necessary (Stokes & Baer, 1977).

Devan is a middle school student with ASD. He writes short phrases and some sentences. Typically his writing is disorganized and readers have difficulty following the flow of his ideas. When presented with a writing task, Devan will write one phrase or sentence and state that he is finished. His language arts teacher, Ms. Rivera, is teaching the class to write persuasive essays. Language arts class consists of a variety of activities (e.g., peer tutoring, brainstorming, peer editing, individual writing time). After Ms. Rivera gives the class a persuasive writing prompt (e.g., Should students be permitted to have cell phones in school?), Devan meets with his cooperative learning group. Students take a position on the issue and brainstorm a list of reasons to support their opinion. One student types the list and provides each teammate with a copy of the list (see Figure 12-2). Then students work individually on their essays.

During individual writing time, Ms. Rivera works one-to-one with Devan. She provides Devan with the persuasive writing prompt, his team's list of ideas, and a paragraph template (see Figure 12-3). She uses a task analysis to teach Devan to write a persuasive paragraph (see Figure 12-4). Devan's goal is to independently complete five out of the seven steps of the task analysis for writing a persuasive essay. During instructional sessions she implements a system of least prompts procedure (Doyle, Wolery, Ault, & Gast , 1988). Ms. Rivera reads the writing prompt aloud and tells Devan to write a persuasive essay in response to this prompt. If Devan does not complete the response listed on the task analysis, Ms. Rivera provides a verbal prompt ("Write a topic sentence that tells your opinion") and a gestural prompt (points to the topic sentence space on the paragraph template) simultaneously. If Devan fails to respond correctly, Ms. Rivera repeats the verbal prompt and models the correct response. Devan repeats the response (i.e, copies the sentence) Ms. Rivera modeled. Ms. Rivera knows from her previous work with Devan that the combination of a verbal and model prompt serves as a controlling prompt because Devan can provide the correct response with this level of support. Ms. Rivera provides specific verbal praise for each prompted and unprompted correct response. Ms. Rivera records an "+" on the data sheet for each response Devan completes independently. She records the prompt level provided for each prompted correct response. Ms. Rivera repeats this process for each step of the task analysis, until Devan writes four sentences.

Twice per month, Ms. Rivera provides Devan with an opportunity to write four sentences in response to a persuasive writing prompt without her assistance. She records the number of steps he is able to complete independently. This provides Ms. Rivera with an opportunity to assess Devan's performance under natural conditions.

Figure 12-2

Idea List

Opinion

I agree _____

OR

I disagree _____

Reasons

1. _____

2. _____

3. _____

4. _____

Figure 12-3

Persuasive Paragraph Template
I think _____
First, _____
Second, _____
In conclusion, _____

Combining Systematic Instruction and Computer-Assisted Instruction

Teachers may also consider the use of technology during writing instruction. The majority of research in writing instruction for students with ASD has involved the use of computer-assisted instruction (CAI). CAI may provide opportunities for students to perform writing tasks while bypassing barriers associated with the fine motor demands of handwriting. Teachers also may select software that reduces the cognitive demand of writing tasks. For example, commercial software is available that provides learners with word banks, picture-word pairings, or word prediction technology (e.g., Clicker, Crick Software, 2005; Pixwriter, Slater & Slater, 1994). Despite the potential for CAI to positively impact student outcomes, it is important to note that the majority of commercially available programs have not been evaluated in the research literature. Therefore, it is critical that software is used as a complement to a strong writing program and not the sole avenue for intervention.

Figure 12-4

Devan's Persuasive Paragraph Template		
Teacher: Rivera	**Instructional cue:** Teacher reads writing prompt aloud and says, "Write a persuasive essay."	
Student: Devan	**Setting:** 3rd Period Language Arts class	**Instructional Method:** System of Least Prompts
Teaching Schedule: M W TH	**Probe Schedule:** Twice monthly (2nd & 4th Fri.)	**Baseline/Probe Method:** Multiple opportunity
Criterion: 5 of 7 steps correct for 4 consecutive trials		**Materials:** persuasive prompt, completed idea list, paragraph, template, pencil, data sheet

Dates	10/1	10/3	10/5	10/8	10/10	10/12	10/15	10/17	10/19	10/22	10/24	10/26
Session Type	B	B	B	T	T	P	T	T	T	T	T	P
Steps												
1. Choose and circle an opinion from your idea list	0	0	+	VG	+	+						
2. Write a topic sentence that tells your opinion	0	0	0	VM	VM	0						
3. Choose and circle a reason from your idea list	+	0	0	VM	+	+						
4. Write a sentence that tells about your first reason	0	0	0	VM	VM	0						
5. Choose and circle a second reason from your idea list	0	0	0	VM	+	0						
6. Write a sentence that tells about your second reason	0	0	0	VM	VM	0						
7. Write a sentence that ends your essay.	0	0	0	VM	VM	0						
TOTAL INDEPENDENT	1	0	1	0	3	2						

Note. **Session type:** B = baseline, P = probe, T = teaching. **Baseline/probe data:** + = correct, 0 = incorrect / no response. **Teaching data:** + = correct, VG = verbal and gestural prompt, VM = verbal and model prompt.

In Figure 12-5 we provide an example of a lesson plan in which the teacher pairs computer-assisted instruction with an evidence-based response prompting procedure called simultaneous prompting. When implementing simultaneous prompting, the teacher asks the student to perform the target behavior while delivering the controlling prompt at the same time. Before each teaching session the teacher conducts a probe in which the student is provided with an opportunity to perform the target behavior without prompting. The teacher records data on the student's performance. The teacher will use these data to determine when to fade prompts. The lesson plan details methods for collecting data and programming for generalization.

Another promising technology used to teach writing skills is video modeling (Delano, 2007a; Kinney, Vedora, & Stromer, 2003). This simple strategy involves recording the student, a peer, or an adult performing a correct writing response and then showing the target student the video immediately prior to the writing activity. (See Chapter 8 for a discussion of video modeling.) Video modeling has been used to teach a variety of skills to students with ASD and has been deemed an evidence-based practice for this population (Delano, 2007b).

Strategy Instruction

In one of the largest studies of writing programs, Graham & Perin (2007) found strong research support for teaching strategies for planning, revising, and editing to struggling writers. A highly effective approach to teaching writing strategies is the self-regulated strategy development (SRSD) model. Over 40 studies of SRSD demonstrate that when this approach is used, students improve their quality of writing, approach to writing, knowledge of writing, and self-efficacy (Harris, Graham, Mason, & Friendlander, 2008). SRSD improves writing skills in children with learning disabilities and attention deficit hyperactivity disorder as well as in writers without disabilities. (See Graham & Perin, 2007 for reviews of this literature.)

Initial studies suggest that SRSD may be effective for students with ASD (Asaro-Saddler & Saddler, 2009; Asaro-Saddler & Saddler, 2010; Delano, 2007a, 2007c). SRSD has been used to teach students with ASD to write stories and persuasive essays, engage in planning and revising, increase the use of action and describing words, and set specific goals for their writing. The results of four studies suggest that students with ASD improve the quantity (number of words written, time spent writing) and quality (number of story elements, number of essay elements, holistic rating) of their writing when the SRSD approach is used.

Figure 12-5

Sample Lesson Plan	
Objective	When presented with a picture of a familiar stimulus, a computer-based word bank, and a verbal request to construct a sentence, Ginevra will construct a simple sentence with 100% accuracy across three consecutive sessions and across 20 different stimuli
Materials	20 pictures of familiar stimuli, Pixwriter (Slater software, 1994), Data Collection Sheets
Procedure	Simultaneous Prompting (Gibson & Schuster, 1992) ***Controlling Prompt:*** (*During SP the same controlling prompt is used throughout instruction*): Gestural (pointing to the correct word on the array). ***Trials per Stimulus:*** During training, the teacher will present five pictures, two times each, for a total of 10 trials.
Data Collection	*Correct Response:* The construction of a simple sentence containing a subject, verb, and adjective. Mark a "+" on the data sheet. *Error:* The construction of an incomplete sentence or a sentence that does not correspond to the pictured stimulus. Mark a "-"on the data sheet. *No Response:* Student does not start a response within 5 s. Mark a "NR" on the data sheet.

Figure 12-5 (continued)

Sample Lesson Plan	
Daily Sessions	*Daily Probes:* Each day, the teacher will present a probe prior to instruction and record the student's response on a prepared data sheet. The teacher will present a pictured stimulus, the computer-based array and say "Write a sentence about the picture." The teacher will wait 10 s for the student to respond. If the student does not respond within 5 s or starts responding and then pauses for 5 s between the selection of a word, the teacher will discontinue the trial and mark an "-" on the data sheet. If the student makes an error, the teacher will ignore the error and present the next trial. If the student constructs a correct sentence, the teacher will deliver verbal praise. *Instruction:* Each day, the teacher will present the pictured stimulus, the computer-based array, and say "Write a story about the picture." The teacher then will immediately point to each word in the targeted sentence and wait for the student to respond. After the completion of the prompted sentence, the teacher will deliver praise.
Generalization	After the student reaches 100% accuracy on the first set of pictures, the teacher will assess the student's ability to write sentences using pencil and paper or a word processor in the absence of the word bank. In addition, the teacher will randomly present untrained pictured stimuli to assess generalization to novel pictures.

The developers of SRSD have published excellent resources that provide detailed descriptions of SRSD teaching procedures. (See the books *Powerful Writing Strategies for All Students*, Harris et al., 2008; and *Writing Better: Effective Strategies for Teaching Students With Learning Difficulties*, Graham & Harris, 2005, that are referenced at the end of the chapter.) Therefore, this section provides a brief overview of SRSD. Teachers implementing the SRSD approach use explicit instruction to teach students strategies for various genres of writing (e.g., story writing, persuasive essay, narrative, expository, report writing) as well as strategies for the writing process (e.g., planning and revising; Harris et al., 2008). Self-regulation strategies such as goal setting, self-monitoring, self-instruction, and self-reinforcement are also part of the SRSD approach. Teachers may conduct strategy instruction in a whole group, small group, or one-to-one context. Teachers use six stages of instruction to teach a strategy: develop background knowledge, discuss the strategy, model the strategy, memorize the strategy, supportive/collaborative practice, and independent performance. Teachers may modify the order of the stages or combine stages to meet students' needs (Harris et al., 2008). Though the SRSD approach provides a structure for instruction, it is flexible enough to allow for individualization. Given the structured approach of SRSD and the incorporation of self-regulation, teachers may find SRSD to be a very good match for some students with ASD.

Conclusion

The recommendations made in this chapter should serve as mere guidelines for planning writing instruction for students with ASD. There are a variety of strategies available for teaching writing and we encourage educators to evaluate the effectiveness of these strategies with the struggling writers in their classrooms. In conclusion, we have two recommendations. First, we recommend that in the absence of evidence-based practices for teaching writing to students with autism, teachers proceed with caution by delivering instruction in the context of continuous data collection and by adjusting their instruction if their students do not progress. Second, teaching academic skills such as writing and providing access to the general education curriculum to all students requires strong collaboration between special educators, general educators, support staff, and families. Research suggests that students with ASD can acquire a variety of writing skills. The challenge for practitioners and researchers is to identify effective instructional methods that will increase communication and writing skills for students across the autism spectrum.

References

Asaro-Saddler, K., & Saddler, B. (2009). The effects of a self-regulated writing strategy on the story writing ability of a young student with autism. *Intervention in School and Clinic, 44*, 268-275.

Asaro-Saddler, K., & Saddler, B. (2010). Planning instruction and self-regulation training: Effects on writers with autism spectrum disorders. *Exceptional Children, 77*, 107-124.

Crick Software. (2005). Clicker 5 [Computer software]. Westport, CT: Author.

Delano, M. E. (2007a). Improving written language performance of adolescents with Asperger syndrome. *Journal of Applied Behavior Analysis, 40*, 345-351.

Delano, M. E. (2007b). Video modeling interventions for individuals with autism. *Remedial and Special Education, 28*, 32-42.

Delano, M. E. (2007c). Use of strategy instruction to improve the story writing skills of a student with Asperger syndrome. *Focus on Autism and Other Developmental Disabilities, 22*, 252-258.

Doyle, P. M., Wolery, M., Ault, M. J., & Gast, D. L. (1988). System of least prompts: A literature review of procedural parameters. *Journal of the Association for the Severely Handicapped, 13*, 28-40.

Gibson, A. N., & Schuster, J. W. (1992). The use of simultaneous prompting for teaching expressive word recognition to preschool children. *Topics in Early Childhood Special Education, 12*, 247-267.

Graham, S., & Harris, K. (2005). *Writing better: Effective strategies for teaching students with learning difficulties.* Baltimore, MD: Brookes.

Graham, S., & Perin, D. (2007). A meta-analysis of writing instruction for adolescent students. *Journal of Educational Psychology, 99*, 445-476.

Harris, K., Graham, S., Mason, L., & Friendlander, B. (2008). *Powerful writing strategies for all students.* Baltimore, MD: Brookes.

Kinney, E. M., Vedora, J., & Stromer, R. (2003). Computer-presented video models to teach generative spelling to a child with an autism spectrum disorder. *Journal of Positive Behavior Interventions, 5*, 22-29.

National Commission on Writing. (2004, September). Writing: A ticket to work… or a ticket out: A survey of business leaders. Retrieved from http://www.writingcommission .org/prod_downloads/writingcom/writing-ticket-to-work.pdf [Context Link].

Pennington, R. (2009). Exploring new waters: Writing instruction for students with autism. *Beyond Behavior, 19*(1), 17-25.

Slater, J., & Slater, J. (1994). Pixwriter [Computer software]. Guffy, CO: Slater Software.

Stokes, T. F., & Baer, D. M. (1977). An implicit technology of generalization. *Journal of Applied Behavior Analysis, 10,* 349-367.

Additional Resources

Graham, S., & Harris, K. (2005). *Writing better: Effective strategies for teaching students with learning difficulties.* Baltimore, MD: Brookes.

Harris, K., Graham, S., Mason, L., & Friendlander, B. (2008). *Powerful writing strategies for all students.* Baltimore, MD: Brookes.

Slater, J., & Slater, J. (1994). Pixwriter [Computer software]. Guffy, CO: Slater Software.

Teaching Mathematics to Students With High Functioning Autism

Peggy J. Schaefer Whitby

Mathematics is one of the most challenging areas of the school curricula for students with disabilities, including students with autism spectrum disorders (ASD). Researchers have noted that nearly 25% of children with ASD meet criteria for a mathematics learning disability (Mayes & Calhoun, 2006). Many of these children demonstrate average performance related to early mathematics skills that involve rote memorization (Chiang & Lin, 2007); however, as mathematical material transitions to a greater emphasis on conceptual understanding, a decrease in performance is noticed (Whitby & Mancil, 2009). Strengths in rote acquisition (Mayes & Calhoun, 2003a) and procedural knowledge sometimes result in the appearance of high mathematical ability, especially in the early years (Whitby & Mancil, 2009), which may delay appropriate intervention.

Currently, evidenced-based strategies to teach mathematics to children with high-functioning ASD are limited (Lord & McGee, 2001). Traditionally, children with ASD have been taught using direct instruction, discrete trial training, or Touch Mathematics (Bullock, 1991) approaches. Direct instruction has been effective in increasing discrete skills such as identifying numbers, rationale counting, memorization of mathematical facts, and memorization of mathematics procedures (Cihak & Foust, 2008; Taubman et al., 2001). However, direct instruction procedures may not build the conceptual knowledge that leads to success in high-level mathematics such as applied problem solving. Students with ASD have difficulty with conceptual knowledge and applied problem solving across all domains (Goldstein, Minshew, & Siegel, 1994). The National Council for Teachers of Mathematics (NCTM) stresses problem solving as a main goal of mathematics for all students across five skill areas: numbers and operations, algebra, geometry, measurement, data analysis, and probability (NCTM, 2000). Most state and district mathematics goals mirror those of the NCTM. Thus, students with ASD need to move beyond rote memorization of mathematics facts to the development of conceptual understanding to achieve at the same level as their peers.

The purpose of this chapter is to present an instructional model and specific methodology to help children with high-functioning autism or Asperger's syndrome (HFA/AS) develop conceptual knowledge in mathematics (i.e., deepen understanding of the meaning associated with mathematical symbols and procedures). Specifically, the Explicit Instruction Model will be described and recommended as a means for teaching important mathematics concepts using the concrete-representational-abstract teaching sequence and/or cognitive strategies. Although additional research related to the use of these instructional approaches with students with HFA/AS is needed, preliminary findings suggest these methodologies fit the unique cognitive profile of students with HFA/AS.

Explicit Instruction Model

Over the past two decades, mathematics reform efforts have supported instruction in which students construct knowledge by interacting with mathematical materials, representing ideas and processes in different ways, sharing ideas with other students, making connections between classroom and real world problem solving, and developing deep conceptual knowledge (NCTM, 2000) through inquiry-based or student-mediated learning (Scheuerman, Deshler, & Schumaker, 2009). Although inquiry-based instruction may build strong conceptual knowledge for typically developing learners, students with HFA/AS may struggle because inquiry-based learning requires the use of executive functions that have been identified as weaknesses for these individuals. Executive functioning involves (a) memory/planning (which includes cognitive processes such as organization, working memory, and interference control), (b) set shifting/mental flexibility, (which includes cognitive process such as perseveration, attention, self-monitoring, weak central coherence) and (c) inhibition/response control (which includes cognitive process such as impulse control; Happe, Booth, Charlton, & Hughes, 2006). These learning characteristics are common for students with HFA/AS and clearly have the potential to effect mathematics performance. Perhaps one way to reconcile the apparent gap between inquiry-based mathematical procedures and the deficits that are characteristic of students with HFA/AS is to adapt and merge evidence-based practices for teaching mathematics to students with disabilities with some aspects of inquiry-based methodology.

The Explicit Instruction Model represents a practical approach for facilitating a merger between evidence-based practices and inquiry-based methodology for teaching mathematics to students with HFA/AS. Explicit instruction is teacher-directed, systematic, and structured. This type of instruction involves the use of a four-phase teaching sequence: advanced organization, demonstration, guided practice, and independent practice (Hudson, Miller, & Butler, 2006). The Explicit Instruction Model can be merged with an inquiry-based model. When students grapple with a concept and struggle with concept mastery, explicit instruction can be used. Explicit instruction guides concept development while allowing the learner to actively engage in the process.

The Explicit Instruction Model (see Table 13-1) has the potential to support the learner with HFA/AS by limiting the impact of executive-functioning deficits during the learning process. This model also can be used in conjunction with evidence-based methodology such as the concrete-representational-abstract approach and strategy instruction, and to increase the conceptual understanding of learners with HFA/AS.

Concrete-Representational-Abstract Approach

The purpose of the Concrete-Representational-Abstract (CRA; see Table 13-2) approach is to build conceptual knowledge prior to learning the procedures or rules for solving mathematics problems. Conceptual understanding is exhibited through four different cognitive processes (Hudson & Miller, 2006): application, noting relationships, transformation, and transfer (Cathcart, Pothier, Vance, & Bezuk, 2000). Application is demonstrated by applying previously learned information to new situations or problems. Noting relationships is demonstrated by the ability to identify connections between mathematical functions. Transformation is demonstrated by the ability to take one problem form and represent it in another form. Transformation includes the ability to restate the mathematical problem in other words using different language. Transfer is the ability to use the mathematical idea or concept in a different context than it was originally taught. Students who are able to demonstrate the four cognitive processes are better able to think and communicate mathematically (Hudson & Miller, 2006). Students with HFA/AS have difficulty developing conceptual understanding due to their cognitive deficits (Barnhill, 2000; Goldstein et al., 1994; Griswold, et al., 2002; Mayes & Calhoun, 2003a, 2003b; Minshew, Goldstein, Taylor, & Siegel, 1994). The concrete-representational-abstract teaching sequence has the potential to assist students with conceptual understanding in spite of these deficits. Concrete instruction involves the use of manipulative devices to illustrate a mathematical concept. Students do the math with the manipulative devices providing a clear concrete level of understanding. Once the concrete level is mastered, students are introduced to the representational level by showing how each piece of the concrete model can be represented with a picture, drawings, or tallies.

Representational instruction involves several lessons on the use of pictures or drawings that represent the concept being taught. Once students master the representation level, instruction progresses to the abstract level. This level includes the use of numbers only until the student is able to demonstrate a concept without the aid of manipulative devices or drawings. The Explicit Instruction Model can be used at each phase of CRA instruction. The use of the Explicit Instruction Model will assist the learner in making connections between the three levels of instruction.

Table 13-1

Explicit Instruction and High-Functioning Autism or Asperger's Syndrome		
Phases of the explicit teaching cycle[a]	Summary: Implementing the Explicit Teaching Cycle[a]	Theory Behind Suggested Use
Advanced Organizer	Prepare for Learning 1. Review prior knowledge 2. State current lesson objectives 3. Guide students in linking past learning with new learning.	Students with ASD have difficulty with generalizing information and connecting prior learning in new contexts.
Demonstration	Model to Develop Understanding 1. Model the activity using think aloud to demonstrate cognitive and meta-cognitive processes. 2. Engage students with questions and prompts. 3. Adjust demonstration or re-demonstrate to make clarifications based upon student understanding.	1. Teach to the student's visual strengths. 2. Allows for students to witness teacher's mental processes through think aloud. 3. Demonstration can serve as a prime.
Guided Practice (Hudson, Miller & Butler, 2006)	Support Learning 1. Assist students with the development of new concept by providing a high level of support including verbal prompts for each step. 2. Gradually fade level of support as students demonstrate proficiency. 3. Question students to monitor performance. 4. Give positive and corrective feedback.	1. Working memory deficits may make it difficult for the student with ASD to manipulate multiple pieces of information at one time. 2. Weak central coherence may make it difficult for the student with ASD to understand the concept without linking the details.. 3. Preference for detail and routine may make it easy for the student with ASD to remember the steps or details in the task.

Table 13-1 *(continued)*

Explicit Instruction and High-Functioning Autism or Asperger's Syndrome		
Phases of the explicit teaching cycle[a]	**Summary: Implementing the Explicit Teaching Cycle**[a]	**Theory Behind Suggested Use**
Independent Practice	Maintenance of learning provides opportunities for independent practice when the student has demonstrated proficiency. 1. Vary the format of independent practice to maintain student interest. 2. Formats can include computer, worksheets, games, peer and cooperative groups	1. Students with ASD may need multiple practice opportunities. 2. Students with ASD may benefit from checklists or visual supports to keep their attention for task completion. 3. Students with ASD may need frequent checks and positive reinforcement for task completion.

Note. ASD = autism spectrum disorders. [a] The information identified with an [a] is adapted from the following authors' research: *Strategic Math Series: Level 2*, by S. Miller, B. Kaffar, and C. D. Mercer, 2011. Copyright 2011 by S. Miller, B. Kaffar, and C. D. Mercer.

In summary, the CRA approach presents students with a concrete and a visual representation of mathematical problems, which assists students in understanding what the mathematics problems actually mean (e.g., multiplication means groups that contain the same quantity of the same items; addition means combining two quantities to obtain a larger quantity). CRA helps students with HFA/AS make connections between rote/procedural knowledge and conceptual knowledge by building the cognitive processes that support conceptual learning in mathematics. Furthermore, visual structures in the concrete and representational format present an abstract concept in a more concrete fashion (Griffin, Griffin, Fitch, Albera, & Gingras, 2006), allowing students with HFA/AS to use their visual strength to bring meaning to abstract concepts.

Table 13-2

	Concrete-Representational-Abstract Approach for Students With High-Functioning Autism or Asperger's Syndrome	
Phases of the CRA[a]	**Summary: Implementing the CRA Strategy[a]**	**Theory Behind Suggested Use**
Concrete	Modeling 1. Teacher models the problem with concrete materials (blocks, chips, pattern blocks, fraction bars, etc.). 2. Teacher guides students in modeling problems with concrete materials. 3. Student demonstrates the ability to model problems with concrete materials.	1. Students with HFA/AS may be strong visual learners. 2. Allows student to "do" the problem before abstracting. 3. Allows students to build application and demonstrate concepts in mathematics.
Representational	Demonstration 1. Teacher demonstrates how the concrete materials can be represented at the semi-concrete level. Semi-concrete models can include circles, tallies, or dots. 2. Teacher links each step of the concrete model to a matching representational model. 3. Teacher guides students in setting up semi-concrete models of the concrete materials. 4. Students demonstrate the ability to represent concrete mathematic problems with tallies, drawings, etc.	1. Students with HFA/AS have difficulty with connecting concepts or generalization of concepts. 2. Students with HFA/AS have difficulty with abstractions so may need a semi-concrete representation to build up to abstraction. 3. Helps build *transformation* as students are representing the problem in another form.

Table 13-2 *(continued)*

Concrete-Representational-Abstract Approach for Students With High-Functioning Autism or Asperger's Syndrome		
Phases of the CRA[a]	**Summary: Implementing the CRA Strategy**[a]	**Theory Behind Suggested Use**
Abstract	Linking 1. Teacher links the concrete, representation to an abstract representation. Abstract representation includes numbers, notations, or mathematical symbols. 2. Teacher links each step in the abstract model to both the concrete and representational model of the mathematical problem. 3. Teacher guides students in setting up abstract models of the concrete and representations of the mathematical problem. 4. Student demonstrates the ability to represent concrete and representational mathematical problems with mathematical symbols.	1. Students with HFA/AS have difficulty with abstractions. 2. Helps students with HFA/AS build connections between the C-R-A, and bring meaning to the abstract. 3. Further builds transformation as students learn to represent mathematical concepts with symbols.

Note. HFA/AS = High-Functioning Autism or Asperger's syndrome; C-R-A = Concrete-Representational-Abstract. [a] The information identified with an [a] is adapted from the following authors' research: *Strategic Math Series: Level 2,* by S. Miller, B. Kaffar, and C. D. Mercer, 2011. Copyright 2011 by S. Miller, B. Kaffar, and C. D. Mercer.

Strategy Instruction

Another teaching methodology that supports the acquisition of important mathematics skills is strategy instruction. Strategy instruction is used to teach the rules, processes, and steps that are applied systematically to obtain a problem solution (Simpson, 2005). Cognitive strategies are the thinking skills that good problem solvers use to solve problems accurately. Meta-cognitive strategies are the processes of self-monitoring when and where to apply specific strategies (Pressley & Harris, 2006). Students with HFA/AS may need to be taught specific strategies for problem solving especially related to solving word problems (Barnhill et al., 2000). Additional research is needed to determine the effectiveness of strategy instruction for students with HFA/AS, but preliminary findings are positive. Specifically, *Solve It!* Problem Solving Routine was found to increase the percentage correct on multiple step word problems for students with HFA/AS (Whitby, 2009).

The Solve It! strategy (see Table 13-3) involves a series of steps designed to help students solve mathematical word-problems (Montague, 1996, 2003). The strategy consists of both cognitive and meta-cognitive steps. The cognitive steps are read, paraphrase, visualize, hypothesize, estimate, compute, and check. Within each cognitive step, the meta-cognitive steps of say, ask, and check are embedded. The instructional model used to teach this strategy integrates the Explicit Instruction Model and includes four components: (a) assessment; (b) explicit instruction; (c) process modeling; and (d) evaluation including error analysis, strategy maintenance, and generalization (Montague, 2003). The assessment identifies students who need word problem solving instruction, provides a baseline to compare progress, and allows the teacher to begin error analysis to determine needs. Explicit instruction brings a depth of understanding to the lessons by linking real world importance and prior knowledge in an advanced organizer and using a graduated teaching model that begins with teacher demonstration to independent mastery. Process modeling is provided in a demonstration. The teacher not only demonstrates the problem, but also models the process through think aloud. Modeling shows the students the cognitive and meta-cognitive process that the teacher uses to solve the problem. Evaluation guides instruction and provides the teacher with information on what needs to be re-taught, practiced and reinforced, or has been mastered. Generalization is the ability to use the strategy in other settings and under different circumstances. By providing multiple opportunities to use the strategy in different settings and in different circumstances, the teacher is training for generalization.

Table 13-3

Solve It! Routine for Word Problem Solving		
Cognitive/ Meta-Cognitive Strategy[a]	**Implementation[a]**	**Support for Suggested Use**

Read for understanding.
 	
Paraphrase–Say it in your own words.
 	
Visualize–Draw a picture or diagram.
 	
Hypothesis–Devise a plan.
 	
Estimate–Round up or down.
 	
Compute–Do the math.
 	
Check–Compare to estimate. Redo the computations.
 	
(Montague, 2003)
	Step 1:
	Assessment (Montague, 2003)
	    Implement Mathematical Problem Solving Pre-Assessment to determine need for intervention.
	Step 2:
	Teach strategy using an explicit teaching model.
	A. Advanced Organizer
	    Link learning objective to real world.
	B. Demonstration
	    1. Model the activity using think aloud to demonstrate cognitive and meta-cognitive processes.
	    2. Engage students with questions and prompts.
	    3. Adjust demonstration or re-demonstrate to make clarifications based upon student understanding.
	    4. Demonstrate for at least three teaching sessions or until all students have memorized the steps in the strategy.
	C. Guided Instruction until students have achieved 80% Mastery
	    1. Gradually fade support as students demonstrate proficiency.
	    2. Question to monitor performance.
	    3. Give positive and corrective feedback.
		1. Teach to the student's visual strengths (Mayes & Calhoun, 2003). Students with HFA/ AS have strength in visual processing (Mayes & Calhoun, 2003a,b, 2008). Visualize step presents an abstract concept in a more concrete fashion (Griffin et. al, 2006).
		2. Break word problem solving into manageable components (Mayes & Calhoun, 2008). Students with HFA/AS may need organizational support for complex materials (Mayes & Calhoun, 2008). Solve It! provides organization to multiple step word problems.
		3. Students with HFA/AS may have difficulty with comprehension (Mayes & Calhoun, 2003a,b). Paraphrasing may support students' comprehension.
		4. Students with HFA/AS have difficulty with complex planning (Happe et. al, 2006). The hypothesis step provides students with structure to developing a plan.
		5. Students with HFA/AS have difficulty with self-monitoring and response inhibition (Happe et al., 2006). The Check step provides a process for self-monitoring.

Table 13-3 (continued)

Solve It! Routine for Word Problem Solving		
Cognitive/ Meta-Cognitive Strategy[a]	*Implementation[a]*	*Support for Suggested Use*

	D. Independent Practice
	  1. Provide weekly opportunities for independent practice.
	  2. Conduct error analysis on independent practice work samples.
	  3. If student achievement goes below 80%, conduct a refresher lesson.
	
	Step 3:
	Post-Assessment (Montague, 2003)
	A. Implement Mathematical Problem Solving Post-Assessment
	B. If student achievement is below 80% conduct error analysis and determine appropriate instructional support level
	C. Continue teaching Solve It! at the adjusted instructional level.
	
	Step 4:
	Generalization (Montague, 2003)
	A . Embed Solve It! in all mathematical word problem solving across the curriculum.
	B. Provide modeling, guided practice and independent practice across the curriculum.	

Note: HFA/AS = High-Functioning Autism or Asperger's syndrome. The information identified with an [a] is a summary of the following author's research: *Solve it! A practical approach to teaching mathematical problem solving skills,* by M. Montague, 2003, Reston, VA: Exceptional Innovations.

Students with HFA/AS frequently present with good declarative and procedural memory, however, they demonstrate difficulties with conceptual knowledge (Solomon, Ozonoff, Cummings, & Carter, 2008) and information processing for complex tasks such as solving word problems (Goldstein et al., 1994; Griswold et al., 2002; Minshew et al., 1994). It appears logical that the executive-functioning deficits in students with HFA/AS (Happe et al., 2006) interfere with the ability to (a) organize and plan steps to solve complex problems, (b) monitor and self-regulate responses for multiple step problem solving, and (c) use the mental flexibility needed to update and manipulate information in working memory for complex problem solving. Strategy instruction provides structure and routine to complex cognitive tasks (Simpson, 2005), which may assist students with HFA/AS in compensating for the executive functioning deficits that interfere with solving mathematical word problems.

Conclusion

Children with HFA/AS need support to develop conceptual knowledge in mathematics. This type of knowledge is necessary to understand and generalize the meaning associated with mathematics computation and word problems. Although research in this area is in its infancy, it appears that the Explicit Instruction Model involves the use of instructional procedures that may help address the unique needs of students with HFA/AS. It also appears that instructional methodologies that have been validated for the learning disability population (i.e., CRA and Strategy Instruction) may help meet the unique needs of students with HFA/AS in terms of increasing the conceptual knowledge in mathematics. Additional investigations related to the Explicit Instruction Model (Hudson, Miller, & Butler, 2006), the CRA (Hudson & Miller, 2006; IRIS Center, 2004), and *Solve It!* (Montague, 1996, 2003) are needed to evaluate and refine these interventions for students with HFA/AS. Additional research is also needed to determine meaningful ways to merge these practices with the inquiry-based techniques advocated through NCTM and routinely used in general education classes that include students with HFA/AS (NCTM, 2000).

References

Barnhill, G., Hagiwara, T., Smith Myles, B., & Simpson, R. L. (2000). Asperger's syndrome: A study of the cognitive profiles of 37 children and adolescents. *Focus on Autism and Other Developmental Disabilities, 15,* 146-153.

Bullock, J. K. (1991). *Touch math addition.* (4th ed.). Colorado Springs, CO: Innovative Learning Concepts.

Cathcart, W. G., Pothier, Y. M., Vance, J. H., & Bezuk, N. S. (2000). Learning *mathematics in elementary and middle schools.* Upper Saddle River, NJ: Merrill.

Chiang, H., & Lin, Y. (2007). Mathematical ability of students with Asperger syndrome and high-functioning autism. *Sage Publications and the National Autism Society, 11,* 547-556.

Cihak, D., & Foust, J. (2008). Comparing number lines and touch points to teach addition facts to students with autism. *Focus on Autism and Other Developmental Disabilities, 23,* 131-137.

Frith, U., & Happe, F. (1999). Theory of mind: What is it like to be autistic? *Mind and Language, 14(1),* 1-22.

Goldstein, G., Minshew, N. J., & Siegal, D. J. (1994). Age differences in academic achievement in high-functioning autistic individuals. *Journal of Clinical and Experimental Neuropsychology, 16,* 671-680.

Griffin, H. C., Griffin, L. W., Fitch, C., Albera, V., & Gingras, H. (2006). Educational interventions for individuals with Asperger syndrome. *Intervention in School & Clinic, 41,* 150-155.

Griswold, D. E., Barnhill, G. P., Smith Myles, B., Hagiwara, T., & Simpson, R. (2002). Asperger's syndrome and academic achievement. *Focus on Autism and Other Developmental Disabilities, 17,* 94-102.

Happe, F., Booth, R., Charlton, R., & Hughes, C. (2006). Executive function deficits in autism spectrum disorders and attention-deficit/hyperactivity disorder: Examining profiles across domains and ages. *Brain and Cognition, 61,* 25-39.

Hudson, P., & Miller, S. P. (2006). *Designing and implementing mathematics instruction for students with diverse learning needs.* Boston, MA: Pearson Education.

Hudson, P., Miller, S., & Butler, F. (2006) Adapting and merging explicit instruction within reform based mathematics classrooms. *American Secondary Education, 35(1),* 19-32.

Iris Center. (2004). Concrete-representational-abstract instructional approach. *The Access Center: Improving Outcomes for All Students K-8.* Retrieved from http://iris.peabody.vanderbilt.edu/

Lord, C., & McGee, J. P. (Ed.). (2001). *Educating children with autism.* National Research Council, Division of Behavioral and Social Sciences and Education. Washington, DC: National Academy Press.

Mayes, S., & Calhoun, S. (2006). Frequency of reading, math, and writing disabilities in children with clinical disorders. *Learning & Individual Differences, 16,* 145-157.

Mayes, S., & Calhoun, S. L. (2003a). Analysis of the WISC-III, Stanford-Binet: IV, and academic achievement test scores in children with autism. *Journal of Autism and Developmental Disorders, 33*, 329-341.

Mayes, S., & Calhoun, S. L. (2003b). Ability profiles in children with autism. *Sage Publications and The National Autism Society, 6*(4) 65-80.

Mayes, S., & Calhoun, S. L. (2008). WISC-IV and WIAT-II profiles in children with high functioning autism. *Journal of Autism and Developmental Disorders, 38*, 428-439.

Miller, S. P., Kaffar, B.J., & Mercer, C.D. (2011). *Subtraction with regrouping, strategic math series: Level 2.* Lawrence, Kansas: Edge Enterprise.

Minshew, N .J., Goldstein, G., Taylor, H. G., & Siegel, D. J. (1994). Academic achievement in high functioning autistic individuals. *Journal of Clinical and Experimental Neuropsychology, 16*, 261-270.

Montague, M. (1996). Assessing mathematical word problem solving. *Learning Disabilities Practice, 11*, 238-248.

Montague, M. (2003). *Solve it! A practical approach to teaching mathematical problem solving skills.* Reston, VA: Exceptional Innovations.

National Council of Teachers of Mathematics. (2000). *Principles and standards for school mathematics.* Reston, VA: Author

Pressley, M., & Harris, K. R. (2006). Cognitive strategy instruction: From basic research to classroom instruction. In P. Alexander & P. Winne (Eds.), *Handbook of educational psychology* (2nd ed., pp. 265-286). San Diego, CA: Academic.

Scheuerman, A. M., Deshler, D. D., & Schumaker, J. B. (2009). Effects of the explicit inquiry routine on the performance of students with learning disabilities on one-variable equations. *Learning Disabilities Quarterly, 32*, 103-119.

Simpson, R. (2005). *Autism spectrum disorders: Interventions for youth and children.* Thousand Oaks, CA: Corwin Press.

Solomon, M., Ozonoff, S. J., Cummings, N., & Carter, C. (2008). Cognitive control in autism spectrum disorders. *International Journal of Developmental Neuroscience, 26*, 239-247.

Taubman, M., Brierley, S., Wishner, J., Baker, D., McEachin, J., & Leaf, R. (2001). The effectiveness of a group discrete trial instructional approach for preschoolers with developmental disabilities. *Research in Developmental Disabilities, 22*, 205-219.

Whitby, P. J. S. (2009). *The effects of a modified learning strategy on the multiple step mathematical word problem solving ability of middle school students with high-functioning autism or Asperger's syndrome.* (Unpublished doctoral dissertation). University of Central Florida, Orlando, FL.

Whitby, P. J. S., & Mancil, G. R. (2009). Academic achievement profiles of children with high functioning autism and Asperger syndrome: A review of the literature. *Education and Training in Developmental Disabilities, 44,* 551-560.

Williams, K. (1995). Understanding the student with Asperger's syndrome: Guidelines for teachers. *Focus on Autistic Behavior, 10,* 1-8.